East End MURDERS

From JACK THE RIPPER to RONNIE KRAY

East End MURDERS

From JACK THE RIPPER to RONNIE KRAY

NEIL R. STOREY

The History Press

First published 2008

The History Press Ltd
The Mill, Brimscombe Port
Stroud, Gloucestershire, GL5 2QG
www.thehistorypress.co.uk

British Library Cataloguing in Publication Data.
A catalogue record for this book is available from the British Library.

ISBN 978 07509 5069 5

Typesetting and origination by The History Press Ltd.
Printed in Great Britain

CONTENTS

ACKNOWLEDGEMENTS

The author would like to express his gratitude to the following: above all my thanks go again to Stewart P. Evans for his enduring friendship, knowledge and generosity. It would be remiss of me not to thank the wonderful Rosie too for her kind and thoughtful hospitality. Again it has been a pleasure and privilege to meet such fascinating people while indulging in some of the darkest research; I would particularly like to acknowledge Don Rumbelow for his advice on the chapter 'Blood on the Streets'. I would also like to thank Tower Hamlets Local Studies Library, Whitechapel Library, Dr Stephen Cherry, Colin and Rachel Stonebridge, Les Bolland, Clifford Elmer Books, Philip Hutchinson, Robert 'Bookman' Wright, Elaine Abel, Great Yarmouth Library and of course my dear family, beloved Molly and son Lawrence for their support and love for this author and his research.

INTRODUCTION

In this volume I shall be taking you on a journey through the history of murder in the East End. Tragically murder, manslaughter, accidents and suicides have brought death to these streets on many occasions, be it wrought in the pursuit of crime – perhaps a theft, a rape, a robbery gone wrong – or perhaps during a drunken brawl; some of these crimes are bizarre, vengeful, gross, debauched, mad or just plain bad. All happened here. I do not attempt to retell every one of them but I have chosen what, I trust you will find, are a selection of the more fascinating cases, from the Regency period to the Swinging Sixties, every one of them infamous, some of them terrifying the populace in their day and all of them with some curious aspects and twists of fate or horror to intrigue the modern reader.

So often while I pursue and investigate the stories of crime in the nineteenth and early twentieth century I would like to be able to travel back in time and ask a question, examine the site for myself before time changed it beyond recall and talk to the investigating officers. When considered in contrast to the long scale of history these cases are often, frustratingly, fairly recent. We can be fairly certain visits were made by criminologists in the days, years or decades after the crimes while events were still in living memory, but these visits are seldom recorded... but I have found one.

Come back with me to 19 April 1905, when a young barrister named S. Ingleby Oddie met up with his friend Dr Gordon Brown at the Police Hospital, Bishopgate. Oddie was allowed to bring some friends with him, and the entire party consisted of Sir Arthur Conan Doyle, Professor Churton Collins, Harry Brodribb 'H.B.' Irving, Dr Crosse and three detectives from the City of London Police. Thus were gathered together some of the finest crime writers and medical experts of their day – who then embarked upon a tour of the Jack the Ripper murder sites led by Dr Brown, the man who had conducted the post-mortem on Catherine Eddowes. He also examined the body of Alice Mackenzie, and took part in the investigation into the Pinchin Street torso, accompanied by detectives well versed in the case. Tragically one can only imagine the conversation as the group made their journey around the murder sites little changed since the blood first ran across the cobbles in 1888; however, in his book *Inquest* (1941), Oddie did record his impressions of the places they visited and undoubtedly reflected some the comments and impressions shared by the other members of the group:

> The scenes of the murders all presented one common characteristic. They were all dark and obscure and secret as possible. Nearly all of them, however, were evidently selected as being places from which it would be easy to slip away unobserved. In Buck's Row for example there were easy alternative exits. In Mitre Square there were no less than five. In Hanbury Street, the scene was the back yard of a common lodging-house, approached by a passage giving a ready exit into any one of three neighbouring backyards, and thence into the street... Miller's Court in Dorset Street seemed to be a trap, yet one had to remember that in this case the Ripper went into the victim's own single room instead of conducting his operations, as in other cases, in the open street. This latter place was a dismal hole seen on a dark, wet, gloomy afternoon. It consisted of one very small room, with a very small window, a fire, a chair and a bed. It was sombre and sinister, unwholesome and depressing, and was approached by a single doorstep from a grimy covered passage leading from Dorset Street into a courtyard. Indeed, it would be just the sort of mysterious and foul den in which one would imagine dark, unspeakable deeds would be done. Yet it was only a stone's throw from the busy Whitechapel Road. It was here Mary Kelly was done to death... I saw the police photograph of the mass of human flesh which had once been Mary Kelly, and let it suffice for me to say that in my twenty-seven years as a London Coroner I have seen many gruesome sights, but for sheer horror this surpasses anything I ever set eyes on.

It was to be almost seventy-five years before that same dread picture was seen by the British public for the first time. In this book that now-infamous photograph is reproduced and accompanied by the transcriptions of the post-mortem examinations of the bodies of the other victims. When reading these reports it is hardly surprising that these killings stood out as different, even to East End residents and police who had become hardened to death and murder – they were more explicitly horrible than anything they had ever encountered before. Even in this modern world of criminal profiling so many questions remain unanswered: what was the mental state of Jack the Ripper, for example? Was he truly insane, or was he pretending to be mad? Was he schizophrenic, or a living embodiment of Jekyll and Hyde (a character portrayed on stage by American actor Richard Mansfield at the Lyceum at the time of the murders)? The depiction certainly pricked the darker corners of concern in the minds of upstanding members of Victorian society, perhaps particularly among those who were outwardly respectable but secretly debauched and violent behind closed doors, or at least away from the gaze of decent people... perhaps in the shadows of the East End.

Harry Brodribb 'H.B.' Irving
– actor and notable crime
writer.

What intrigues me is to consider if Jack knew the dark corners of the East End intimately. Could he stalk the streets looking for victims in the most vulnerable places known to him? Did he plan his attacks knowing the escape routes he would use? Or were the warren of back streets and shadowy corners of the East End merely a convenient place to carry out his nefarious deeds, leaving him to get away more through luck than judgement?

Despite attempts to suggest conspiracies and present apparently robust and well-researched theories about who Jack was and why he committed the murders, I do not believe that after this distance of time we will ever be able to conclusively prove this or that person was Jack the Ripper – but I don't think we will stop looking for him either. So I present the lion's share of this volume as an overview of the Jack the Ripper crimes, the most infamous murders in history. But, dear reader, do not neglect the other tales in this volume; terror and infamy were nothing new to the East End.

Walk with me to the Ratcliff Highway and read of a series of horrible murders –
and consider if you think the man accused of the killings acted alone. Meet Henry
Wainwright, pillar of Whitechapel society, with two wives and two families – one
public, one very private. When the cost of his high living caught up with him, one
of them had to go. Then, after our main investigation of Jack the Ripper, there is
the case of tragic Frances Coles, who had her throat slashed in the dingy tunnel
passageway known as Swallow Gardens – was she another victim of Jack the Ripper?
Other murderers in this volume include the infamous William Cronin – but should he
have hanged in 1897 rather than 1925?

Further cases from the twentieth century put the darkest side of life in the East End on
the covers of the world's press – including the Houndsditch Murders, which led to the
infamous Siege of Sidney Street. Armed pursuits on foot and by all manner of vehicles
took place, bullets rattled through the air, civilians were caught in the crossfire and brave
police officers fell in the line of duty, all of which culminated in a siege which drew
attention and comments from the international press.

The final story sees the close of a chapter in the East End's history. The Krays
were violent hard men of the East, but they knew 'their manor' and abided by a
certain 'code' among felons and between rival gangs. Despite both being murderers,
their killings were seen as gangland actions against those who grossly transgressed
'the code', and with their smart suits and high profile, fostered by a series of iconic
photographs, the Krays caught the imagination of the wider public. When they died
they were given a 'full East End honours' send off and thousand lined the streets to
watch the funeral cortège pass.

Neil R. Storey
2008

1

THE RATCLIFFE HIGHWAY MURDERS

1811

The Ratcliffe Highway runs from East Smithfield to Shadwell High Street. In *Old and New London*, Walter Thornbury wrote:

Ratcliffe Highway, now called St George Street, is the Regent Street of London sailors, who, in many instances, never extend their walks in the metropolis beyond this semi-marine region. It derives its name from the manor of Ratcliffe in the parish of Stepney … The wild beast shops in this street have often been sketched by modern essayists. The yards in the neighbourhood are crammed with lions, hyenas, pelicans, tigers. As many as ten to fifteen lions are in stock at any one time, and sailors come here to sell their pets and barter curiosities.

J. Ewing Ritchie was far less flattering when he said in *The Night Side of London* (1858):

I should not like a son of mine to be born and bred in Ratcliffe-highway…(there) vice loses all its charms by appearing in all its grossness. I fear that it is not true generally to the eyes of the class she leads astray, that:

> Vice is a monster of such hideous mien,
> That to be hated, needs but to be seen.

Exotic animals may be one fascination, the darker corners of the street the haunt of whores, harpies and footpads, but the Ratcliffe Highway was tainted with blood and infamy years before.

At about midnight on the night of Saturday 7 December 1811 a certain Timothy Marr (24), a wholesale mercer dealing in lace and pelisse at 29 Ratcliffe Highway, sent his servant girl, Margaret Jewell, out to buy some oysters for supper and pay the bill from the baker. As Jewell left the Marr's, Mrs Celia Marr was suckling their

The Ratcliff Highway, renamed St George's Street, pictured around 1896, described as 'the Regent Street of London sailors' and scene of the most notorious early nineteenth-century murders in the capital.

fourteen-week-old baby, Timothy junior, while Mr Marr was preparing to close his shop. Jewell found the oyster dealer had closed: she tried elsewhere but could find no oysters for sale, so she went to the baker to pay the bill. After about twenty minutes the girl returned and rang the bell, but received no answer. No lights were apparent in the building. Wondering what could have happened, she listened at the keyhole and believed she could hear 'a foot on the stairs and I thought it was my master coming to let me in; I also heard a child cry in a low tone of voice. I rang then again and again, and knocked at the door with my fist.'

Margaret was clearly distressed so George Olney, a nightwatchman who called the time every half hour and knew the Marrs, came over to enquire what was going on. He also knocked on the door and called out to Marr through the keyhole, but received no response. Olney had good reason to be concerned. At midnight he had passed the shop and spoken to Marr and apprentice Gowan as they were shuttering up the shop. On his return he had noticed one of the pins in the iron crossbar of the window shutters was loose. He rapped on the door and called out what he had found, and was answered by what he thought was a strange voice, that said, 'That's alright.' Unperturbed, at least at that time, Olney walked on, but now those events troubled the watchman.

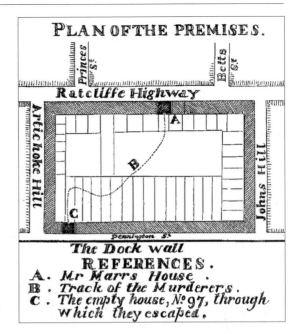

A contemporary map of the scene of the Marrs' murder.

Next-door neighbour John Murray, a pawnbroker, was woken by the commotion and shouting. He got up and went to the shop front, where Jewell explained that she had been locked out. Hearing what Olney had to say, Murray decided to investigate. He climbed over the dividing wall between his yard and the Marrs'. Once in their yard he was attracted by a light on the landing place and discovered the back door was open. He took the light and – with some trepidation – entered the building. He first encountered the body of the shop apprentice James Gowan (14) lying dead in a pool of blood and gore on the floor and, as stated in the *Newgate Calendar* (1818), 'with his brains knocked out, and actually dashed, by the force of the murderous blow, against the ceiling.'

Murray called out for help and made his way to the street door, where he discovered Celia Marr laying face down, dreadfully wounded and lifeless. He let Watchman Olney in and together they searched for Timothy Marr. They found him behind the counter, blood still oozing from his hideously battered head. They then went to the kitchen, where, as the *Newgate Calendar* continues; 'petrified with horror they saw the little babe in the cradle, with one of its cheeks entirely knocked in with the violence of a blow, and its throat cut from ear to ear.'

The watchman sounded the alarm by springing his rattle, a hue and cry was raised and the Thames River Police were soon on the scene; the first officer present was Charles Horton. The findings of the investigation of the murder were reported before the magistrates of the Shadwell Police Office. A search of the house first revealed a long iron ripping chisel, about 20in in length, but this had no stains of blood upon it. However, the next tool, a ship carpenter's maul, with an iron head 'somewhat in the shape of an anvil' – and broken at the point – was found covered with fresh blood and a few hairs.

The bloodstained ship's carpenter's maul used in the murders at the Marr household.

As two sets of tracks were discovered in the yard, it was deduced that there must have been two attackers. The footprints were of two different sizes and the heels turned to the rear of the houses as if running away. The footsteps were marked with sawdust and blood – the sawdust had been caused by carpenters working in the shop during the day. It was thought the killers had come into the shop under the pretence of purchasing goods, as it was clear Marr had been reaching down for some stockings when he had been struck. No money was found missing from the till and cash to the tune of £160 was found about the house.

Within hours a number of arrests were made (mostly of sailors who had been in the area during the hours in question), but each suspect had a solid alibi and was released – and soon the public were all too aware that two killers were on the loose. As the horrific details of the murders circulated by word of mouth, in the press and on lurid broadsides, the people of London were said to have been gripped by fear. Macaulay recalled the state of panic in London, 'the terror which was on every face; the careful barring of doors; the providing of blunderbusses and watchmen's rattles. We know of a shopkeeper who on that occasion sold 300 rattles in about 10 hours.'

Handsome rewards were offered for the apprehension of the killers. The day after the crimes, by order of the churchwardens, overseers and trustees of the Parish of St George, John Clerk the vestry clerk rapidly published bills headed: 'FIFTY POUNDS REWARD: HORRID MURDER!!' Stating the circumstances of the murders and weapons used, they asked that, 'Any person having lost such articles, or any dealer in old iron, who has lately sold or missed such are earnestly requested to give immediate information,' offering the reward of £50 for the discovery and apprehension of the person or persons responsible – 'to be paid on conviction.'

On 9 December the magistrates of the Thames Police Office in Wapping repeated the offer of a reward on their bill, and appealed for information appertaining to three men seen loitering near Mr Marr's shop for about half an hour on the night in question, one of them during that time looking in at the shop window. It gave the following description:

One of them was dressed in a light coloured sort of Flushing coat, and was a tall lusty man; another was dressed in a blue jacket, the sleeves of which were much torn, and

Reward poster for the capture
of the perpetrator of the Ratcliff
Highway murders.

under which he appeared to have also flannel sleeves, and had a small rimmed hat on his head. Of the third no description has yet been obtained.

The Thames Police added a further reward of £20 for the person responsible for the identification or apprehension and commitment of the murderers.

The inquest into the murders was held on Tuesday 9 December before the coroner, William Unwin Esq., at the Jolly Sailor public house, which was situated nearly opposite the Marr's house; a large crowd lingered outside until about 2 p.m., when the jury began to assemble, and watched with curious expectation as the coroner led the jury to the Marr's house, where they inspected the scene of the crime and viewed the bodies of the victims.

Mr Walter Salter, a surgeon in the Parish of St George, reported the findings of his examination:

Timothy Marr, the younger: the left external collected artery divided, the left side of the mouth laid open, with a wound 3in in length [remember that this was inflicted on a 14-week-old baby, so it was hardly surprising the initial reports thought the baby's throat was cut from ear to ear] and several marks of violence on the left side of the face. Celia Marr: the left side of the cranium fractured, the temporal bone totally destroyed, with a wound just above the articulation of the jaw 2in in length, then winding into the left ear, and a wound at the back of the ear. Timothy Marr, the elder: the nose broken, the occipital bone fractured, and a violent blow on the right eye. James Gowan [also spelt Gowen and Goen]: several contusions on the head and nose, with the occipital bones dreadfully shattered, and the brains protruding.

The coroner gave a short address to the jury on the known facts of the case and after a short deliberation returned a verdict of 'Wilful Murder against some person or persons unknown' on each of the bodies.

After the inquest the bodies of the Marr family were laid out on beds in their home and the public were allowed to go through the house and view them. Hundreds passed through the room and saw the corpses, displayed with their horrific wounds unsutured and their eyes left open. The Marr's were finally buried on Sunday 15 December, mother and child in one coffin, Mr Marr in another; the mourners, more curious members of the public than grieving friends and family, lined both sides of the route – and were many rows deep – from 29 Ratcliffe Highway to the door of St George's-in-the-East.

Thames Police Office published another bill detailing a clue found on the maul – the letters I.P. (other accounts state an alternative of J.P.), 'in dots on the crown, near the face, [which appear] to have been so marked with a coppering punch.' More suspects were arrested: even Marr's brother-in-law was questioned, but all to no avail as solid alibis were provided.

The fear on the streets was palpable, and further rewards were offered on bills by private gentlemen and, significantly, by the Government: first £100, then £500 – a veritable fortune in 1811. But then the murderers struck again.

Shortly after 11 p.m. on the night of Thursday 19 December, the neighbourhood of Old Gravel Lane, Ratcliffe Highway rang with the cries of 'Murder!' Crowds gathered as an almost nude man lowered himself from the window of a tall building at No. 81 – the King's Arms public house – and dropped the last few feet into the arms of a passing watchman. The young man was John Turner, an apprentice who boarded at the pub, who cried out, 'They are murdering the people in the house!'

The landlord and his wife had run the pub for about fifteen years and were well liked in the area, so when people heard the cry of 'Murder!' they wanted to help, and set about hammering on the doors of the pub. Constable Hawse and some men from the crowd – including a butcher from Ashwell's buildings named Ludgate – forced an entry through the cellar-flap and entered the building. At the same time another man, named Fox, cutlass in hand, managed an entrance through some wooden bars at the side of the house.

In the cellar the body of Jack Williamson (56), the landlord, lay at the foot of the stairs, his legs on the stairs, his head down. A horrific blow had been inflicted on his head and his throat dreadfully cut. An iron crowbar lay by his side. The men made their way upstairs into the parlour where they found Jack's wife, Mrs Elizabeth Williamson (60), and the servant girl, Bridget Harrington. Their skulls had been smashed in and their throats cut, blood still issuing from the wounds. As the men searched the house from room to room, they discovered Kitty Stillwell, the Williamson's granddaughter, still in her bed, alive and untouched. Although the house had been completely surrounded almost from the moment the alarm was raised, the murderers had somehow managed to escape.

John Turner's escape from the window of the King's Arms, taken from a contemporary booklet.

At the subsequent inquiry before the Shadwell Police Officer Magistrates the escapee, John Turner, gave his account of events inside the pub on that fatal night:

I went to bed about five minutes before eleven o'clock; I had not been in bed more than five or ten minutes before I heard the cry of 'We shall all be murdered', which I suppose was the cry of the woman servant. I went downstairs, and I saw one of the villains rifling Mrs Williamson's pockets, and I immediately ran upstairs; I took up the sheets from my bed and fastened them together, and lashed them to bed-posts; I called to the watchman to give the alarm; I was hanging out of the front window by the sheets; the watchman received me in his arms, naked as I was.

At the coroner's inquest, held at the Black Horse tavern, just across the road from the King's Arms, he enlarged on his account. Turner said he had entered the pub around 10.40 p.m. and gone to his room on an upper floor. He heard Mrs Williamson lock the door. Then he heard the front door bang open 'hard', and Bridget shout, 'We shall all be murdered!' Mr Williamson was then heard to say, 'I am a dead man!' The sound of several blows followed, and then the sound of someone walking about with shoes in which, he believed, there were no hobnails. After a few minutes, he arose and went to see what had occurred. He heard three drawn-out sighs. As he crept downstairs, Turner saw a door standing open with a light burning on the other side. Peering inside, he saw a tall man leaning over Mrs Williamson. Turner estimated him to be 6ft tall and believed he was wearing a Flushing coat. The man appeared to be going through Mrs Williamson's pockets.

Fearing for his own life, he turned and fled back up to his room, tied two sheets together and lowered himself out of the house. Next to nothing appeared to have been taken from the pub but Turner had noticed that Mr Williamson's watch was missing. Turner also pointed out he had no recollection of an iron bar in the pub such as the one that was found beside Mr Williamson – it must have been brought there by the killer.

On Monday 23 December an Irish sailor named Williams was apprehended on suspicion of being involved in the murders and brought before the magistrates. He was known to frequent the Williamson's pub – in fact, he had been there on the night in question. When he was arrested he was found to be in possession of £1 and a considerable amount of silver, even though a sailor who shared his lodgings at the Pear Tree recalled that Williams had complained he was short of money. Williams claimed he had obtained this money, which was a considerable sum in its day, from pawning some of his clothes. The most damning evidence, however, came from the silent witness – the maul which had been used to viciously batter the Marr household to death.

Williams had lodged with Mr Vermilloe. A seaman at the same lodging, a ship's carpenter by trade, had left some of his tools there for safekeeping, but upon inspection the maul was found to be missing. The seaman's name was John Peterson, and all his tools were marked with his initials, 'J.P.' Comparison between the initials on the maul and the other tools proved a match. At the time of the hearing Mr Vermilloe was unfortunately imprisoned for debt, so the magistrates went with the maul to Newgate. Vermilloe immediately recognised the tool as the one which had been left with him by Peterson and even remembered how the maul's end had broken when he was breaking up some firewood. At the hearing other witnesses, when they could stand a close examination of the gory exhibit, confirmed it was the one left by Petersen and that they had not seen it for about a month.

On the second day of the hearing, held on Tuesday 24 December, John Turner was brought in as a witness. Although he had seen Williams in the pub on a number of occasions, he could not say on oath that Williams was the man he had seen rifling through Mrs Williamson's pockets.

Mrs Rice, the sister-in-law of Mr Vermilloe – who also worked as a washerwoman and was Williams landlady – stated she had washed for the prisoner for about three years, but, 'on Friday last fortnight I washed a shirt of his which was very much torn about the neck and breast, and had a good deal of blood upon it, about the neck and arms.' She had thought Williams had been fighting, and had washed his clothes in a similar state before. Williams said the blood and tears to the clothing had been caused during a scuffle with some Irish coal-heavers after a card game at the Royal Oak. Another witness, John Richter, who shared the lodging house with Williams, had noticed the accused had shaved off his sandy-coloured whiskers, which had once formed such a 'striking feature' of Williams' appearance – an event also considered strange by Mrs Vermilloe.

On Friday 27 December 1811 Williams was due to be examined before the Shadwell Police Court. The crowd, hoping for a glance of Williams, had been gradually growing in number outside the court since the early hours of the morning, the streets buzzing with opinions, theories and stories. The court was ready, and the bloodstained maul and ripping chisel were on a table ready to confront the prisoner, but the crowd was to be frustrated. The officers who had been despatched to collect Williams from Cold Bath Fields Prison and escort him to the hearing returned empty-handed: Williams had been found dead in his cell. As the *Newgate Calendar* explains, he had: 'suspended himself by his neck handkerchief from a projecting piece of wood [some other accounts state an iron bar], which was introduced into the wall for the purpose of hanging his bedclothes on.'

Because Williams was never tried, an air of mystery surrounds the case. It is possible more than one man was involved in the Ratcliffe Highway slayings, but no further suspects were brought to trial after the suicide of Williams; accounts from that time seem to be satisfied to state: 'it was the general opinion, that he was the *only* person concerned in the murders.' However, this conclusion is far too simple and neat for some – what, for example, of the three men (one presumably Williams) seen peering into the Marr's shop? The 'mystery' was further fuelled as magistrates sought to incontrovertibly prove Williams was the killer. The wounds on the throats of the victims were thought, by the surgeons who examined the bodies, to have been inflicted by a razor, but police searching Williams room in January 1812 claimed to have found a sharp knife with bloodstains upon it. Was this the final proof of Williams' guilt, or was it planted there by the police and conveniently 'discovered' to bring the matter to a close?

Irrespective of whether his guilt could be proved, Williams' cadaver faced the same treatment as any suicide. Until the 1850s people who committed suicide could not be buried in consecrated ground, but rather in a separate, distant area on the north side of the churchyard. If they were lucky, the grave would be dug in such a way

Cold Bath Fields Prison, viewed from near Grays Inn Road, *c*. 1820. This is how John Williams would have known the prison for the short time he was held there before his suicide.

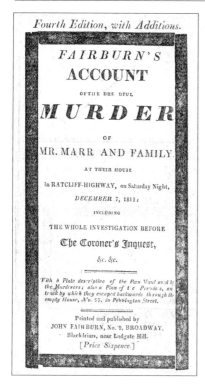

Title page of the fourth edition of
Fairburn's account of the murders
on the Ratcliff Highway, *c.* 1812.

that the body would face west. Many believed that the ghostly spirit of the suicide
would walk abroad with malevolent intent towards those left behind in the land of
the living; such a character as Williams stood no chance of being treated mercifully,
particularly as the mob had been denied a good 'swinging' at Tyburn.

Shortly after 10 p.m. on Monday 30 December, Williams' body was formally
collected from Cold Bath Fields Prison by a party consisting of Mr Robinson, the
High Constable of the Parish of St George; Robinson's deputy, Constable Machin;
and Mr Harrison, the man charged with the task of moving the body. Put into a
hackney coach, the body was taken to the St George's watch-house – known as 'The
Roundabout' – at the bottom of Ship Alley on Ratcliffe Highway and deposited in
'the black hole' until the following morning.

Soon after 9 a.m. the following morning, the High Constable arrived at the watch-
house with attendants and a cart specially fitted with a high platform set at an angle on
top to allow the 'greatest possible degree of exposure' of Williams' body. The fatal maul
was placed in a perpendicular posture on the left side of his head and the ripping chisel
in the same manner on the opposite side; about his head was the iron crowbar found
beside Mr Williamson. A stake sharpened at the extreme end and destined to be used
on Williams was placed in the same direction between the head and the shoulders. The
corpse, escorted by the High Constable, civic dignitaries and Mr Gale, Superintendent
of Lascars in the East India Co.'s Service, mounted on horses (along with constables,
headboroughs and the patrols of the parish with drawn cutlasses – and the Beadle of

The body of John Williams on the cart specially fitted with a high platform set at an angle on top to allow the 'greatest possible degree of exposure' as it was escorted through the streets to the crossroads at St George's Turnpike – where he was buried with a stake driven through his heart.

St George in his official dress), was driven to the Marrs' house, before stopping for about ten minutes at the King's Arms, where the Williamsons were murdered. The crowd were recorded as 'issuing smothered groans' as the macabre display passed along the route. Finally, the procession, corpse and all, arrived at a section of what was then New Road at St George's Turnpike where Canon Street Road and Cable Street, in St George-in-the-East, crossed over each other. Here, two men mounted the cart, removed Williams' body, 'and unceremoniously hurled the remains of the monster into its last earthly receptacle, amidst the acclamations of the surrounding spectators.' The grave was not quite long enough for Williams' body to fully recline so it was 'crammed down in rather a contracted position' and subjected to the old crossroad burial 'rite' of 'pinning' in the form of a stake being driven through the heart (a practice only prohibited by an Act of Parliament in 1823). The event was made more piquant by the fact that the stake was hammered in by the same maul which had been used to kill the Marrs. A quantity of unslacked lime was then thrown into the hole and the rest filled in with earth. The paving stones were then restored to their original position.

But still the body of John Williams was not allowed to rest. When works were carried out for The Commercial Gas Co. in 1886, a trench was dug for pipe-laying, and, at a depth of 6ft, the skeletal remains of Williams were uncovered, 'the stake still clearly evident' between his ribs. His bones were then unceremoniously divided up between relic collectors and souvenir hunters around the area. His skull was displayed at a nearby pub.

2

THE BUSINESSMAN, THE ACTRESS & THE DISMEMBERED MISTRESS

Henry Wainwright, 1875

And, long since then, of bloody men,
Whose deeds tradition saves;
Of lonely folks cut off unseen,
And hid in sudden graves;
Of horrid stabs, in groves forlorn,
And murders done in caves.

And how the sprites of injured men
Shriek upward from the sod.
Ay, how the ghostly hand will point
To show the burial clod:
And unknown facts of guilty acts
Are seen in dreams from God!

From *The Dream of Eugene Aram* by Thomas Hood (1799–1845)

The East End of London is a place of many contrasts, perhaps none greater and more visible than the juxtaposition between rich and poor; the wealthy on Whitechapel Road living cheek-by-jowl with some of the poorest and most marginal people in the land. Henry Wainwright was one of the fortunate ones. He had grown up in an affluent family where his father, a respectable tradesman, was a pillar of society in business and public life and a church warden of the parish. When he died he left the handsome sum of £11,000 to be divided between his four sons and one daughter. Henry and his brother Thomas went into partnership running a brush-making business with a shop at No. 84 Whitechapel Road and a warehouse almost opposite at No. 215; they had contracts to supply the workhouse and even the Metropolitan Police. To all outward appearances Wainwright was a typical Victorian gentleman and lived with his wife and children in the smart Georgian Tredegar Square in the Mile End district of the London Borough of Tower Hamlets. Indeed, it was said of Wainwright that, 'At the beginning of the year 1874 there was probably no more popular or respected individual among the principal inhabitants of that long and broad thoroughfare, the Whitechapel Road, than Mr Henry Wainwright.' So wrote Henry Brodribb Irving in his introduction to *Trial of the Wainwrights* in the respected *Notable British Trials* series (1920). As ever, Irving summed the man up impeccably; to the society around him Wainwright was known for his generous bonhomie, his prominent work with the Christchurch Institute at St George's-in-the-East, charity work, recitations at educational establishments, ardent support for the Conservative party, patronage of the theatre and social suppers. Indeed, he had a reputation for lavish entertaining, and for actors on very humble salaries it was a much-desired privilege to be asked out to supper with Mr Wainwright. The East-End tragedian J.B. Howe wrote of a chance encounter with Wainwright in his book *A Cosmopolitan Actor*; after being recognised by Wainwright, Howe was invited to his house, met his family and shared a drink, some entertaining stories and even a cab. As they jumped into the vehicle, Howe noted the affection with which Wainwright bade farewell to his family, kissing the children and his wife. Howe was to recall, 'I thought I had never in my life encountered a nicer man.' In the light of subsequent events it was somewhat ironic that Wainwright's own favourite recitation after social suppers was Hood's *Dream of Eugene Aram* (a notorious eighteenth-century case of deception and violent robbery which resulted in murder and the hiding of the corpse): those who saw the performances of this poem recalled Wainwright performing it 'with force and vigour but without that peculiar sense of horror which makes its recitation so vivid in the hands of a great actor.' Perhaps their opinions were far more perceptive than the audience realised: in fact, it was not his acting ability which lacked, but rather his own deep-seated callousness that revealed itself through his performance.

Wainwright was often to be found at the Pavilion Theatre, which was next to his shop at No. 84 Whitechapel Road. He was there on the night Arthur Orton, 'The Tichborne Claimant', came to raise funds for his approaching trial (a campaign Orton undertook between the years 1873–4 to finance a legal case which gained national notoriety as the longest trial in English legal history, in which Orton attempted to maintain his claim on the Tichborne family name and fortune. In fact, he was a butcher from Wagga-Wagga who was impersonating the lost son of Lady Tichborne). The account tells how, after Orton had finished his oration, the heavy drop curtain was lowered unexpectedly. Unaware of the danger, Orton, who was immediately under the drop, could have been seriously injured had not a man from the audience leapt to his feet and pulled him out of danger. This dramatic act of gallantry was met

Wainwright's warehouse at
No. 215 Whitechapel Road.

with thunderous applause and the 'claimant' and his rescuer appeared in front of the curtain – hand-in-hand – to receive the audience's appreciation. The hero that saved Orton was none other than Henry Wainwright.

But Henry Wainwright was not all he seemed. He lived a double life. He was, by the standards of the 1870s, where our story really begins, an attractive man of average height, broad shouldered in build, who sported a fine head of dark brown wavy hair, full and penetrating blue eyes and a cultivated beard behind which was concealed 'a heavy and sensual mouth' blessed with wit and fine conversation. Among women he was considered to have a certain air of exoticism and no little mystery such as might be attached to an aesthete; all gifts he used to full effect as he charmed and conquered a string of attractive young ladies – or at least that is what he would have liked those to whom he told his tales to believe.

One young lady to fall for Henry Wainwright's charms was Harriet Lane, whom he met at Broxbourne Gardens, a popular pleasure resort for Londoners at that time on the banks of the River Lea. They soon became intimate and announced their marriage as the union between Percy King (the almost laughable phallic pseudonym of Wainwright) and Harriet Lane in February 1872, and thus the beguiled girl in her early twenties became Mrs Harriet King went to live with her 'husband' in a comfortable house on St Peter's Street, Mile End. In the August of 1872, a daughter was born to them, and after a few moves to Alfred Place, Bedford Square and Cecil Street, Strand, Mrs King returned again to St Peter's Street, where a second daughter was born in December 1873.

Pillar of society:
Henry Wainwright *c.* 1875.

Harriet Lane, or rather,
'Mrs Percy King' –
Wainwright's secret wife.

And so the double life of Henry Wainwright might well have carried on, perhaps *ad infinitum*, if his extravagances and *bonhomie* had not taken such a toll on his finances.

Early in 1874 it had become apparent that Henry Wainwright had stretched himself too far and he was facing a financial crisis. He owed his brother William a large sum of money – he could see the danger and dissolved the partnership. Wainwright took on a new partner, but his debts continued to spiral and amounted to well over £3,000 (excluding the money he owed his brother). His creditors met and agreed to accept Wainwright's offer to repay them 12s in the pound. He never paid more than 9s.

Wainwright was thus unable to support his secret second family in the style to which they had become accustomed. Harriet had been given an allowance of £5 a week and was quite happy – she proclaimed she was 'kept like a lady' – but now, little by little, the allowance diminished and she was forced to consider herself, quite rightly, as being of 'reduced circumstances'. She had to give up the St Peter's Street house and take up lodgings at the house of a Mrs Foster at 3 Sidney Square, Mile End Road.

Wainwright's two worlds began to collide when Harriet, frustrated by her lack of financial support, took to visiting Wainwright's shop at 84 Whitechapel Road and making 'unpleasant scenes'. Wainwright could see his upright and respected façade about to be destroyed by Harriet's outbursts, and the whole sordid situation exposed for all society to gossip and dissect. His vanity and pride, made all the more sensitive through his pecuniary situation, could not allow this to happen. On one occasion Wainwright was seen to become violent with Harriet. He had tired of her and despised her for her loyalty to him. She would not be palmed off to another man, Wainwright had no money to pay her off, and rather than have his clandestine activities exposed and face being ostracised by his family and society he decided to rid himself of Harriet once and for all.

On 10 September 1874 Wainwright ordered half a hundredweight of chloride of lime which was delivered to 84 Whitechapel Road. The following day Harriet King left her lodgings at 4 p.m., taking with her a nightdress done up in a small parcel. She told her friend Miss Wilmore she was off to see Wainwright at his shop on Whitechapel Road.

On that same evening of Friday 11 September 1874 three workmen employed near Wainwright's warehouse at 215 Whitechapel Road claimed they heard three pistol shots fired in quick succession between 5 p.m. and 6 p.m. At the time they did nothing more about what they heard. The lime disappeared and Harriet Lane, 'Mrs King', was never seen alive again.

Later, Miss Wilmore became concerned about Harriet and went to see Wainwright. He explained she had run off to live on the continent with a man named Edward Frieake. Soon Miss Wilmore received a letter, purporting to come from Harriet (in reality written by Wainwright's brother Thomas), in which she said she wanted nothing more to do with Mr King, her family or friends. Further telegrams purporting to come from Harriet were also received. Harriet's friends were not entirely convinced and sought out Edward Frieake, who turned out to be an auctioneer and friend of Wainwright. He knew nothing of Harriet Lane or a Mrs King. When Wainwright was challenged about this he claimed the Edward Frieake who had run off with Harriet was a different man who simply shared the same name. Did her friends believe this remarkable coincidence? If concerns had been passed to the police they certainly were not acted upon in any significant way. Perhaps the memory of Harriet would have gradually faded to the occasional comment of, 'I wonder whatever happened to…' from those who once knew her.

Whatever was generally thought to have happened to Harriet, Henry Wainwright was a changed man. Gone was the hale-fellow-well-met, the *bon vivant*. Frank Tyars, who had performed at the Pavilion, noticed the change in Wainwright: 'Instead of the breezy, self-confident gentleman he had known, he saw a man walking slowly along in a furtive, hang-dog way.' J.B. Howe could not believe the change in his old acquaintance and noted Wainwright 'had become nervous, impatient and irritable. He had taken to visiting public houses, where he would sit drinking more than was good for him, and nervously cracking and eating walnuts, of which he was very fond.' Most believed that Wainwright's personality change was a result of his financial embarrassment, but surely the weight of the murder must have hung heavily and most horribly on his conscience.

By September 1874 Wainwright's business was near collapse and he was obliged to raise money by mortgaging the warehouse at 215 Whitechapel Road. In June 1875 Wainwright was declared bankrupt and in the July the mortgagee of 215 foreclosed and took possession of the premises. But Wainwright was not without friends, and he was lucky enough to count Mr Martin, a well-to-do corn merchant at 78 New Road, Whitechapel, among them. He acquired Wainwright's business, advanced him £300 and even paid Wainwright a salary of £3 a week as manager. But the thought of Harriet still haunted Wainwright – which was hardly surprising considering he had buried her with the quick lime under the floor of the paint room in the warehouse. Some had, over the months since her disappearance, commented on the foul smell at the warehouse, but, because Wainwright had kept his double life so secret, nobody put two and two together.

Perhaps it was because the fateful anniversary of Harriet's murder was approaching, or perhaps because his nerve could simply hold on no more, either way Wainwright wanted her remains out of the warehouse. However, he was in for a shock when he discovered what was left of poor Harriet. No doubt he was expecting the lime to have reacted with her remains and hastened their destruction. This *would* have been the case if Wainwright had bought quicklime (otherwise known as caustic lime, or unslaked lime), however, the chloride of lime Wainwright had bought had worked as a disinfectant and preserved the body!

Despite the split with the business partnership, Henry co-opted his brother, Thomas, to allow him to remove the body to his ironmongery shop premises at the Hen and Chickens at 56 Borough High Street. This arrangement is curious: why should Thomas Wainwright feel compelled to assist his brother hide a murder? And having just had his own business fail, if Harriet's body was hidden in his cellar, how long would it be before they had to remove it again? Whatever the motives (loyalty?

A dramatic representation of Henry Wainwright shooting Harriet Lane on the cover of *Famous Crimes, c.* 1910.

Bribery?), on Friday 10 September the brothers bought a quantity of American cloth, some rope, an axe and a spade. The following morning, a year to the day after Harriet had left her lodgings for the last time, a friend of Thomas Wainwright recalled 'he did not look well' – hardly surprising if one considers the work he assisted his brother with the previous night: Harriet had been dismembered and parcelled up in the American cloth.

Thomas had gone on ahead to his premises; it was thus left to Henry to organise the transportation of the body. Wainwright went to Mr Martin's, where he saw one of the managers, Alfred Stokes. Wainwright undoubtedly trusted Stokes as he had also been in his employ in the brush-making business for about eighteen years. At Wainwright's trial he was to give the following account of the afternoon in question:

> ...about half-past four, when, in Mr Martin's presence he (Wainwright) asked, 'Will you carry a parcel for me, Stokes?' I said, 'Yes sir, with the greatest of pleasure.' We then went together to 215 Whitechapel Road, in through Vine Court to the back premises. Henry took a key out of his pocket and opened the door. We both went in, and he told me to go upstairs and fetch down a parcel. I went upstairs, and through by the skylight... but did not find the parcel. I came downstairs and told him I could not find it; he said, 'Never mind, Stokes, I will find them where I placed them a fortnight ago, under the straw.' I saw

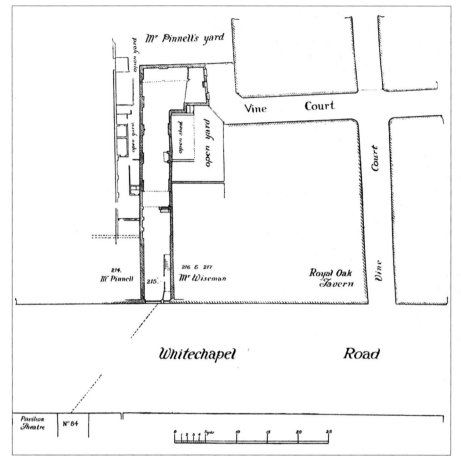

Plan of Whitechapel Road showing the premises at No. 84 and No. 215, occupied by Henry Wainwright.

some straw up in a corner, and two parcels wrapped in black American cloth, and tied up with rope. He said, 'These are the parcels I want you to carry, Stokes.' I lifted them up and I says, 'They are too heavy for me,' and put them down. [Wainwright persuaded Stokes to try again.] I picked up both parcels and followed him. I then said 'I can't carry them; they stink so bad, and the weight of them is too heavy for me.'

Wainwright took the lightest of the parcels from Stokes and they managed to get almost as far as Whitechapel Church, where Stokes begged to rest and appeared to lose his grip a little. Wainwright snapped, 'For God's sake don't drop it, or else you will break it.' When they arrived at the church Wainwright told Stokes to wait with the parcels while he went for a cab. In going for the cab personally, rather than sending Stokes, Wainwright sealed his own fate. While he was gone, Stokes looked in the parcel. Much was made of Stokes' motive for doing so in the press, for the man claimed he had heard 'a supernatural voice which had called to him three times saying, "Open that parcel."'

Alfred Stokes – the man who dared to look in one of the ominous parcels.

The judge anticipated this aspect of Stokes' testimony and cut across him, saying, 'Never mind what you felt you must do. You were asked what you did.'

Stokes stated, 'I looked into the largest parcel. I opened the top of the parcel, and the first thing I saw was a human head. Then proceeding further I saw a hand, which had been cut off at the wrist.'

Stokes closed the parcel and kept his cool as Wainwright brought over a four-wheeled cab. Wainwright lit a cigar while Stokes loaded the parcels and watched the cab set off. He then set off in pursuit, running along behind. At a chemist shop near Greenfield Street, about 70 yards from Church Lane, the cab stopped and Wainwright got out and caught up with a young lady named Alice Day, a ballet dancer he knew from the Pavilion Theatre. She had just come out of a pub on the corner of Greenfield Street and Wainwright asked her if she cared to have a drive over London Bridge. She accepted, so long as she could get back for her evening performance. Puffing on his cigar to mask the foul smell, Wainwright, Alice and parcels set off in the cab – with Stokes in pursuit, vainly trying to attract the attention of two policemen along the way.

The cab reached the Hen and Chickens in Borough High Street, where Wainwright got out before the cab had really stopped. He carried one of the parcels inside. Meanwhile, Stokes had managed to attract the attention of a police officer, PC Henry Turner M48, who came over to the cab and waited for Wainwright to return and walked with him as he carried a second parcel from the cab into the Hen and Chickens. PC Turner asked Wainwright, 'Do you live here?' To which Wainwright replied, 'No.' Turner pressed further, 'Do you have any business here?' Clearly

Thomas Wainwright's premises at the Hen and Chickens, 56 Borough High Street.

agitated, Wainwright retorted, 'I have and you have not.' Turner told Wainwright to 'go inside', but he seemed disinclined to do so. Another constable, PC Cox M290, joined Turner. The policemen lost patience and pushed Wainwright inside.

Wainwright was now left with little option but bribery and begged: 'Say nothing, ask no question and there is £50 each for you.' Cox replied, 'No, we are going to do our duty, and we don't want your money.' By this time Turner had his hands on Wainwright and walked with him down the premises; Wainwright still had the second parcel in his left hand. Cox found one of the parcels Wainwright had brought in lodged in a dark corner at the top of the cellar steps. PC Turner asked Cox to hold Wainwright while he retrieved the parcel and put it on an old counter. Wainwright warned, 'Don't open it, policeman: pray don't look at it; whatever you do don't touch it.' The stench was vile, but investigate he did, by pulling some of the cloth to one side – and in doing so, Turner recalled, 'my fingers then came right across the scalp of a head, across the ear'. Returning Wainwright to the hands of Turner, Cox went to get the cab; Wainwright was desperate and pleaded with the policmen, 'I'll give you £100, I'll give you £200, and produce the money in twenty minutes if you'll let me go.' PC Turner remained unmoved; Wainwright and Miss Day were arrested and taken to Stone's End police station.

On 13 September Henry Wainwright (36) and Alice Day (20) were charged at Southwark Police Court. Depositions were given by Stokes and the constables involved in the arrest. Wainwright remained silent throughout the proceedings until Miss Day clutched hold of him and implored him, 'For God's sake tell them what I

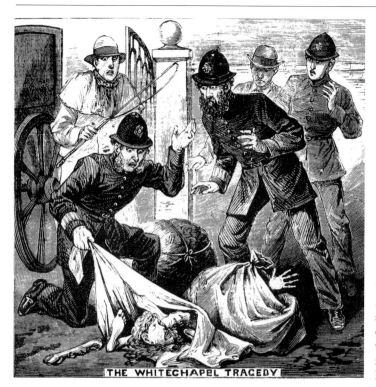

THE WHITECHAPEL TRAGEDY

The Illustrated Police News' sensational depiction of the discovery of the dismembered remains of Harriet Lane.

know of the matter – I know nothing.' Wainwright responded, 'I met her Saturday. She knows nothing.' Both were remanded in custody and brought before the Police Court on 21 September. Alice Day was discharged early on, Wainwright was formally charged with wilful murder. Thomas Wainwright was arrested on 1 October, charged at Southwark Police Court with being an accessory after the fact, and on 13 October both brothers were committed for trial. On 14 October the final judgement of the coroner's jury confirmed the remains were those of Harriet Lane, alias King, and that she was wilfully murdered by Henry Wainwright.

An interesting aside to the proceedings at the Police Court is that Mr Besley, who led the defence for the prisoner, shared the instruction with none other than Mr W.S. Gilbert, who later collaborated with Arthur Sullivan to create the Savoy operas. Gilbert had qualified as a barrister but had given up his practice to concentrate on writing. He had found himself called for jury service at a most inopportune time and discovered to his consternation that only *practicing* barristers were exempted – thus he made this fugitive appearance and claimed his exemption.

The trial of the Wainwright brothers at the Central Criminal Court opened on 22 November before Sir Alexander Cockburn, Lord Chief Justice of England. Sir John 'Sleepy Jack' Holker, the Attorney General, led the prosecution with Mr Harry Poland. The defence for Henry Wainwright was led by Mr Edward Besley with Mr Douglas Strait and Mr C.F. Gill. Counsel for Thomas Wainwright was conducted by Mr Moody.

In the dock at Southwark Police Court, Alice Day implores Henry Wainwright to clear her name.

Sketched from life, Henry (left) and Thomas Wainwright after a week of their trial at the Central Criminal Court.

Despite the Chief Justice, in his opening remarks, speaking of 'the magnitude and importance of this great trial', the truth was that despite the circumstances of murder being both sensational and remarkable, the case was not – the evidence was so clear and unequivocal, the proof of his guilt overwhelming, but still the most senior counsel laboured their speeches, the Attorney General devoting a whole day to his closing speech and the Chief Justice another day for his summing up. The entire trial stretched over nine long days.

The trial finally concluded on 1 December. The jury retired to consider their verdict at 3.45 p.m. After an absence of nearly an hour the jury returned a unanimous verdict of 'guilty' against Henry Wainwright. Thomas Wainwright was found guilty of being an accessory *after the fact* and sentenced to seven years penal servitude. Many who studied the case were to recall Thomas had a near miss: had it not been for the eloquence of his defence he would have undoubtedly faced the same fate as his brother.

Before sentence was passed, Henry Wainwright was asked if he had anything to say. He attempted to enter into a speech but was brought to the point by the Lord Chief Justice. Wainwright acquiesced, saying:

> Then I will imply say that, standing as I now do upon the brink of eternity, and in the presence of that God before whom I shall shortly appear, I swear that I am not the murderer of the remains found in my possession. I swear also that I have not buried these remains, and that I did not exhume or mutilate them as proved before you by witnesses. I have been guilty of great immorality. I have been guilty of many indiscretions, but as for the crime of which I have been brought in guilty I leave this dock with a calm and quiet conscience.

Once sentences were passed on the brothers and they were taken down, the Lord Chief Justice exercised the power vested in him to order a reward, the sum of £30, to be granted to Stokes 'for his conduct and energy… and his perseverance in following up the cab in which those remains were being conveyed [that] in reality led to the discovery of this crime and the conviction of the offender concerned in it.'

Petitions were made for the sentence to be commuted and attempts were made to publicly discredit a witness. *The Times* of Tuesday 21 December reported 'a rumour' that a document written by Henry Wainwright was in the possession of the Home Secretary, the contents of which related:

> That being in pecuniary embarrassment, he grew weary of the importunities of Harriet Lane and the constant drain upon his purse. Harriet Lane had threatened that unless he gave her more money she would expose him to the world as the father of her children, which to a man in his social position meant ruin and degradation. He mentioned these circumstances to his brother Thomas who said he was confident that for a consideration of £20 some man could be got to marry her and take her away.

'He donned the black cap' –
Sir Alexander Cockburn,
Lord Chief Justice of
England, pronounces the
death sentence on Henry
Wainwright.

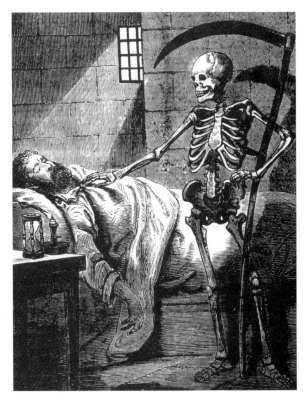

'Wake up Wainwright – you
have an appointment to
keep!' Henry Wainwright
in the condemned cell at
Newgate, just hours before
his execution.

Wainwright went on to claim he paid his brother the money, but Thomas 'went to Henry at 84 Whitechapel Road and said he had got rid of her, and on being asked how, replied that he had shot her.' Henry exclaimed, 'Good God, Tom, what have you done?' He threatened to inform the police, to which Thomas replied if he did so, 'he would swear Henry did it.' She was Henry's paramour and she was laying on his premises, so, in the days before forensics or use of fingerprints in detection, what chance would he have had? So he complied. Thomas was also said to have made a similar statement – except this time it was he who was forced by Henry, the killer, to comply for fear of implication.

On Tuesday 21 December 1875 Henry Wainwright was executed at Newgate Prison by public executioner William Marwood. Wainwright was led out across the yard to the execution shed as the nearby clock of St Sepulchre chimed 8 a.m. Wainwright had clearly dressed with 'scrupulous care', his bearing as he walked demonstrating 'conspicuous fortitude.' A friend of H.B. Irving was present and described the scene to him as:

> absolutely Hogarthian and horrible… the cold December morning, the waning moon, the rope dangling to and fro in the shed awaiting its victim, a gaslight flaring noisily, the well-dressed crowd of privileged visitors (about sixty in number) come to see the show, the Sheriff's footmen, who had some of them obviously fortified their spirits for the occasion; the whole scene seemed ghastly and sickening in the last degree.

Wainwright had been given a special dispensation to smoke a last cigar, which he discarded as he approached the gallows. Looking over his shoulder with a glance of infinite scorn, and then, with a contemptuous movement of his head, he called to those assembled to witness the execution, 'Come to see a man die, have you, you curs!' Speaking no more Wainwright went to his doom with this curse upon his lips. Another who was present noted:

> After the white cap had been drawn over his face and while the noose was being adjusted, the heaving of deep emotion was distinctly visible through the folds of the cap. The necessary preparations were speedily made by the executioner, and all things being in readiness, the drop fell with an awful shock echoing for a moment or two all over the prison yard… Judging from the tension of the rope for some considerable interval after the bolt had been drawn the prisoner must have 'died hard', as the saying goes.

3

TO KILL AN ANGEL

Israel Lipski, 1887

In the year 1887 Batty Street was very much like any other in this predominantly Jewish area of St George's-in-the-East. Although it could not claim to be a street of smart identical terraced houses, contemporary illustrations show a variety of houses of varying heights and typical nineteenth-century construction, quite probably 'jerry built' with tenement occupation in mind, evenly running along the length of the street. Times were hard in that area and it has to be observed with the benefit of hindsight that the area was on the way down – indeed the street is denoted as 'poor' in Booth's survey of 1891.

The problems were further compounded as more and more Jews fled the troubles of Eastern Europe. In *Outcast London*, G.S. Jones states that between 1880 and 1886, 20,000 Jews came to the East End of London. As a result, the tenements in this area rapidly became overcrowded, deprived and unsanitary. In a survey from 1871 only two people were recorded as occupying the three-storey house at 16 Batty Street; by 1887 fifteen people were crammed into the property, among them Isaac and Miriam Angel (22) from Warsaw, who occupied two rooms on the first floor. They had been married for twelve months. Above them on the top floor were two rooms, one of which was occupied by Israel Lipski (22), who had resided at 16 Batty Street for two years. Born a Polish Jew in Warsaw in 1865 named Israel Lobulsk, he changed his name to Lipski shortly after his arrival in London in 1885 and was soon working as an umbrella stick maker and was engaged to his employer's sister-in-law, Kate Lyons. Although the engagement had been broken for some while previously, by June 1887 the betrothal was renewed, Lipski had begun to learn English and had a few savings put away which, after being urged to do so by his future mother-in-law, he had recently drawn out from the bank to set himself up in his own business as a walking stick maker.

On the morning of Tuesday 28 June 1887, Isaac Angel got up early and left for his work as a boot riveter at St George Street, Spitalfields shortly after 6 a.m., leaving his wife, who was six months pregnant, in bed. Miriam was in the habit of visiting her mother-in-law, Mrs Dinah Angel, between 8.30 a.m. and 9 a.m. each day for

A contemporary illustration of Israel Lipski.

breakfast. When she did not arrive Mrs Angel went round to 16 Batty Street to see if anything was wrong, arriving at about 11 a.m. She went directly up to Miriam's room and knocked on the door, but got no response: it appeared to be locked from the inside. Now very concerned, she called down to the landlady, who rushed upstairs with another resident, Mrs Levy. They went up the stairs that led to the attic and, peering through a small side window covered by a muslin curtain, they saw Miriam lying on the bed as if in a faint. The women then rushed to the door, forced it open and ran over to the bed where Miriam lay on her side, her hands behind her and half covered by the bedclothes, her night attire pushed up and 'her person exposed.'

To their horror, the women saw a yellow frothy substance coming from Miriam's mouth and what appeared to be corrosive burns about her head, face, neck and breast. The landlady immediately ran for Dr John Kay, whose surgery was around the corner at 100 Commercial Road. On her way she encountered Dr Kay's assistant, Mr William Piper, and summoned him to the scene. In the meantime Harris Dywein, a general dealer, who knew the Angels, was passing 16 Batty Street at 11.30 a.m. when he heard screams and cries coming from within the house and went to inquire the cause. He saw Miriam on the bed and was there when Mr Piper arrived.

Piper saw that Miriam Angel was dead and recognised the burns about her face as those caused by a corrosive acid. Suspecting foul play, he immediately ushered those present on to the landing and locked the room from the outside. Dr Kay was then urgently summoned. About ten minutes later Dr Kay arrived and the room was again entered. He noted the burns on Miriam's face and hands and agreed with Piper that they were indeed caused by some corrosive substance, probably nitric acid.

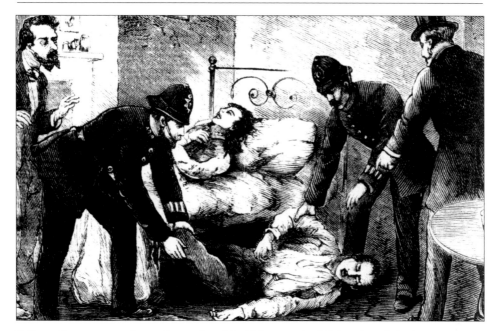

Police officers remove the semi-conscious Lipski from under Miriam Angel's bed.

A search of the room was begun to find the bottle that it had been contained in. It was discovered at the foot of the bed, still containing some of the corrosive liquid, and marked with an almost illegible old label: 'Camphorated Oil: Bell & Co. Chemists, Commercial Road.' Just as the bottle was found, Harris Dywein, who had been feeling under the bed for the lost bottle, leapt back with shock – he had touched a man's hand! Dr Kay pulled the bed from the wall, jumped on it, and, removing a pillow, exclaimed, 'Why, it is a man!' He sent Dywein for the police.

Dywein went to the window and summoned a passing constable, PC Arthur Sack, who was closely followed by PC Alfred Inwood. The man, who was discovered lying on his back, was then brought out from under the bed – it was Israel Lipski, in what appeared to be an unconscious state; his mouth showed evidence of acid burns and his clothes were much burnt from the effects of the same. Dr Kay felt his pulse and exclaimed, 'He is alive.' The doctor then put his finger on Lipski's cornea to see if he was conscious. There was no reaction, so the doctor slapped his face and Lipski opened his eyes.

News soon got out that 'something had happened' and a crowd had gathered in front of 16 Batty Street and around Dr Kay's surgery, anxious to find out what was going on. The police were also soon on the scene and found Lipski's hat on the foot of the bed and his coat under the bed. Lipski himself was extracted from his hide under the bed by the two policemen, as Dr Kay recalled: 'One each side of him – took hold of his arm and pulled him out, the bed was pulled round and he was taken round the end, pulled along the bare floorboards.' He was removed from the house under police escort, through the milling crowd, first to Kay's surgery for further treatment, then to the police station.

SCENE OUTSIDE THE HOUSE.

News soon spread of the murder and a crowd gathered in front of No. 16 Batty Street.

Still believed to be in a precarious position, he was then removed to the London Hospital and placed under a police guard.

Lipski was visited in the hospital by his fiancée, Kate Lyons. She stayed with him for over an hour and when exiting told the press she believed he was innocent and that he was another victim rather than the murderer. By evening, Inspector David Final and Detective Sergeant William Thicke (known to many on both sides of the law as 'Johnny Upright') arrived at Lipski's bedside with an interpreter. He gave the following statement of what had occurred:

At 7 o'clock in the morning a man who had worked for me asked me to give him some work. I told him to wait, that I would buy a vice for him, so that I could give him some work. I went to purchase a vice, but when I got to the shop it was too soon. As I was going along I met another workman whom I knew at the corner of Backchurch Lane. I went back to the shopkeeper, who wanted 4s for the vice, I offered 3s. He said he would not take it. I returned to Batty Street and got into the passage. I then saw the man I had seen in Backchurch Lane. He said, 'Will you give me work or not?' I said, 'Come to the workshop. I am going to breakfast; then I will give you work.' I told my landlady to make some coffee and sent the man to fetch some brandy. I afterwards went upstairs to the first floor. I there saw both these men and saw them open a box. They took hold of me by the throat, threw me down to the ground; there on the ground opened my mouth and poured some poison into it. They said, 'That is the brandy.' They got my hands behind me and asked if I had got any money. I said, 'I have got no more than the sovereign, which I gave you to get the brandy.' They then asked, 'Where is your gold chain?' I said, 'It is in pawn.' They said, 'If you do not give it you will be dead as the woman.' They put

Dr Kay's surgery on the corner of
Commercial Road and Batty Street.

a piece of wood in my mouth. I struggled, and they then put their knees on me against my
throat. One of them said to the other, 'Don't you think he is quite dead yet?' The reply
was, 'Yes, he don't want any more.' They then threw me under the bed and I lay there as
if dead. One of the men I have known by the name of Simon.

The inquest into the death of Miriam Angel opened on the evening of Wednesday
29 June 1887 – while Lipski was still in hospital – at the Vestry Hall, Cable Street,
with Mr Wynne Baxter, Coroner for the County of Middlesex (Eastern District),
presiding. Miriam's body had been removed to St George's mortuary, where Dr Kay
had performed the post-mortem examination the previous afternoon. He presented
his findings at the inquest. Dr Kay had noted 'on the right eye and temple there were
marks of violent blows. There were no other external marks except those of corrosive
poison. On removing the scalp there was evidence of a tremendous blow on the right
temple.' The examination also revealed Mrs Angel must have been on her back when
the acid was administered. 'Both sides of the heart being empty indicated the cause of
death was suffocation from the swallowing of nitric acid.' Dr Kay added, 'there was
something in the vagina which looked like semen, but I could not say for certain if it
is semen without a microscopical examination.' Earlier, when Isaac Angel was asked
via the interpreter if he had recently had intercourse with his wife, a question which
presented the translator with considerable problems phrasing it in Yiddish, Mr Angel
replied that he had not.

   The inquest was adjourned at the request of the coroner to allow Dr Kay to perform
further tests, and opened again on Friday 1 July. Charles Moore of 96 Backchurch
Lane, Whitechapel, the manager of an oilman's shop, gave evidence he sold nitric

acid 'to a man whom he thought he could identify with the man Lipski now lying in the London Hospital.' Dr Kay was recalled and presented his findings, which reveal the woeful inadequacies of forensic tests available to medical examiners in the late 1880s:

> After the last sitting of the inquest I extracted from the vagina of the deceased some matter I found there. I have put it under the microscope. There are no spermatozoa. Had there been any I could have proved it was semen. It might be semen. I agree with the remark of a text book that the semen even of a healthy young man varies much and is scarcely ever twice alike, so that the absence of spermatozoa is no proof that the matter is not semen. There is no other test. I produce a glass bottle with some of the matter taken from the vagina, sealed and marked 'A'.

Dr Kay then related his notes and impressions from the crime scene:

> When I first saw the body of the deceased it was not exposed. The lower part of the body was covered with a feather-bed, and on the upper part there was a shirt, which was unbuttoned, but it did not expose her breasts. On turning the bed down to see if any violence had been offered to her, the legs, thighs, and the whole of her genitals, and the lower part of the abdomen were exposed, and not covered by her chemise. Her thighs were wide apart.

Although the *East London Observer* contained the more graphic accounts of Dr Kay's testimony, most of the national newspapers, such as *The Times*, ever mindful of the sensitivities of their readership, simply recorded Dr Kay's statement as, 'The condition of the deceased caused him to think that an assault had been committed upon her.' Lipski's hospital bed statement was then read out.

Over the two days of the inquest questions were also raised about the relationship between Miriam Angel and Israel Lipski, but none of those asked could say they had even seen Mrs Angel exchange pleasantries with the man.

Lipski was not called as a witness; the telling statement of Inspector Final summed the police view of him: 'Lipski is in custody and would not be produced as a witness if the inquest were adjourned.' The inquest was not adjourned and the jury returned a verdict of 'wilful murder' against Lipski, who was committed to trial on a coroner's warrant.

The following day Lipski was brought before Thames Police Court and committed for trial by Mr Lushington the magistrate. He was then removed to Holloway Prison and transferred to Newgate the week before the trial.

Israel Lipski was first brought before Mr Justice James Fitzjames Stephen at the Central Criminal Court on Wednesday 27 July 1887. The prosecution was the formidable team of Mr Harry Bodkin Poland and Mr Charles Mathews for the prosecution, with Mr Gerald Geoghegan appearing for the defence. The proceedings did not last long. Lipski was asked how he pleaded and replied not guilty 'in a firm

Harry Poland led the prosecution against Lipski. Known for his fairness, Poland had been involved in some of the most significant cases of the late Victorian era, including the Tichbourne Claimant and the Wainwright case.

voice', but Mr Geoghegan requested more time to prepare the defence and asked for the case to be held over until the following Friday. Justice Stephen acquiesced and even suggested that the case may be heard at the next sessions, but Geoghegan declined and the hearing commenced proper on Friday 29 July.

All the learned counsels were immensely experienced legal men; Harry Poland had been involved in some of the most significant cases of the late Victorian era, including the Tichborne Claimant and the Wainwright case. Gerald Geoghegan was one of the leading barristers of his day, but tragically his eloquence was marred by alcohol abuse. A senior counsel, Mr A.J. McIntyre, QC, was brought in over Geoghegan while the trial was held over – perhaps, as Friedland suggests in *The Trials of Israel Lipski*, as Geoghegan was marred by drink again. McIntyre, although a sober and well-respected QC, was not a criminal law specialist and had not appeared at the Central Criminal Court after spending years 'out to grass' on the County Court Bench.

In opening the case, Mr Poland related more about the known movements of Lipski on the morning in question, as recorded in *The Times* of 30 July 1887:

The prisoner was a stick maker, and he had engaged a boy named Pitman and a man named Rosenbloom to assist him in that business. At 6.30 on the morning of Tuesday, 28 June, the prisoner was seen in the yard of the house dressed. The husband of the deceased had gone to work at 6 o'clock. At 7 o'clock Rosenbloom came to work at the house and the boy Pitman at 8 o'clock. The prisoner went to the shop of a general dealer in Backchurch Lane for the purpose of buying a vice and a sponge to be used in his business, and while there he asked what time an oil shop next door opened. Before the prisoner left the house a man named Schmuss called and spoke to the prisoner about working for him. The prisoner told him to go upstairs and wait, which he did for some time, but finding the prisoner did not return, he left. The prisoner went to the oil shop and purchased a pennyworth of nitric acid, which was used in his business. The prisoner returned to the house and asked the landlady to get him some coffee. The coffee was prepared, but as the prisoner was not present the landlady called out to him to come down and get it. The boy Pitman answered that the prisoner was not in his room. It was alleged that at that time the prisoner was in the deceased's room.

In the latter part of the opening, Mr Poland related some of Lipski's statement and soon after brought up as witness Simon Rosenbloom, the 'Simon' accused of being one of those who killed Miriam Angel and attempted to kill Lipski. Under cross-examination from McIntyre, Rosenbloom emphatically denied any involvement in the crime and was clearly believed – to the degree that Mr Justice Stephen took the unusual step of intervening to ask 'whether there was any use in pursing the questions further?'

Mr McIntyre for the defence replied that he was cross-examining Rosenbloom's statement because 'the prisoner could not give his account of the matter.' Mr Justice Stephen, clearly losing patience, replied that he 'had again and again allowed a prisoner to make a statement before his counsel addressed the jury if he wished to do so.'

The other man Lipski had implicated in the murder was named and brought to give evidence at the trial. Isaac Schmuss, as in the case of a number of witnesses, gave his evidence via an interpreter. He denied any involvement in the crime and – despite a suggestion to the contrary by the boy Pitman in his evidence – denied knowing Rosenbloom. Mathews led the questions for the prosecution, and Schmuss openly admitted that he had been to 16 Batty Street on the morning of the murder, at about 8 a.m.; he was hard up and expecting some work from Lipski. He had been met at the door by Lipski and was told to go upstairs and wait. He went to the upper storey room and waited there with Rosenbloom and Pitman. After hanging around for about fifteen minutes the three became fed up with waiting and departed; Schmuss went and had breakfast.

Cross-examination after preliminary questions established Schmuss's trade was that of a slipper maker, and that he could not speak a word of English. McIntyre tried to establish if Schmuss was at the scene of the crime on the morning in question.

McIntyre: Did not you yourself go into the room that belonged to Mrs Angel?
Schmuss: What Mrs Angel? I did not go in.
McIntyre: The first floor in the house where you went to work?
Schmuss: I went nowhere.

McIntyre: Were you not standing in the doorway of her room when Lipski was coming
up the stairs?

Schmuss: No, I was not there. I was nowhere.

McIntyre: You were not with Rosenbloom?

Schmuss: No.

McIntyre: Did you know Rosenbloom?

Schmuss: I saw him once, then I saw him for the first time.

McIntyre: Do you mean that you never saw him till you saw him in Lipski's room?

Schmuss: I saw him never more I saw him the first time there.

The judge was clearly showing his impatience at the line of questioning and McIntyre could sense another intervention coming. He took the initiative by saying: 'My Lord, I do not propose to go through all the same cross-examination as with the last witness, as this man denies being there at all.' Mr Justice Stephen replied: 'No, there is no use in doing that.'

Further witnesses, including Miriam's mother-in-law Mrs Dinah Angel, Harris Dywein, the boy Pitman and the landlady of 16 Batty Street, all recounted their stories of the case. The landlady's evidence was particularly damning. She confirmed, as mentioned in the opening statements of the case, that at about 8.30 a.m. Lipski had asked her to fetch some coffee for him. This she did, but when she called up to let him know it was ready, he did not come; upon a second call Pitman had called back, 'He ain't here.' As she had not see him go out, Lipski's whereabouts in the house were not known between 9 a.m. and the time he was discovered under the bed in Miriam Angel's room.

The second – and what was to prove to be the final – day of the trial opened on 29 July 1887. The first witness called was Inspector Final, who related the circumstances of taking Lipski's statement, after which he read out the tract for the court (including some answers to further questioning by Final during which Lipski expanded his accusation to identify Simon Rosenbloom of Philpot Street as the murderer).

Inspector Final was followed into the witness box by Dr Kay, who gave his account of his first examination and subsequent post-mortem of the body, expanding on his findings to state he considered Miriam Angel had suffered at least four very violent blows, probably from a man's fist, to the right eye and temple, causing her to be, as the doctor phrased it, 'stunned.' The post-mortem revealed the acid, estimated to have been a quantity of about half an ounce, had travelled down to the stomach, leading Kay to deduce 'it had been poured down her throat while she was insensible.' Significantly, Dr Kay was now not inclined to suggest his post-mortem revealed any evidence of recent 'sexual connection.'

Mr William Calvert and Mr Thomas Redmayne, house surgeons at The London Hospital, then gave evidence of Lipski's treatment and injuries. They both confirmed he had swallowed nitric acid: it was found on his clothes and hands. Lipski's hands, right wrist and forearms also bore scratches, but these were not considered by the

Penny Illustrated Paper illustration of items of evidence and the staircase and window associated with the murder.

medical men to 'indicate violence of any serious kind.' Neither was there any visible sign of violence beyond the acid burns and scratches. Then Charles Moore, the manager of the shop in Backchurch Lane, described selling a bottle of nitric acid to a man he identified 'to the best of his belief' as Lipski on the morning of 28 June, and recalled: 'He said he was a stick maker, he wanted it for staining sticks – I cautioned him that it was poisonous.'

The case for the Crown concluded with an appearance from Anna Lyons – the woman who would have been Lipski's future mother-in-law. She recalled lending Lipski money, and when asked about her impressions of the man replied, 'So far I cannot give him a bad character, he always behaved himself.' And with a few questions to further establish Lipski was indeed employing himself as a stick maker (also supplying a list of the names for whom he was known to have worked), her evidence was completed, and all that remained were the counsels' summing up to the jury.

After a recess for lunch Mr Poland presented that facts as:

so simple and clear that on the evidence the jury could form only one conclusion. It was clear that at the time the deceased lost her life she and the prisoner were the only persons in the room, and that on the very day on which the occurrence took place he had purchased the acid which was undoubtedly the cause of death. The question of motive was not material, but upon the facts it was reasonable to suppose that the accused might either have intended to outrage the deceased or to commit a robbery.

Poland then went on to dismiss the allegations of the involvement of Rosenbloom and Schmuss.

Mr McIntyre for the defence said it was his 'painful duty to have to put forward a defence which implicated others [Rosenbloom and Schmuss]', suggesting that two men could have easily overwhelmed Mrs Angel – one administering the blows while the other muffled her cries. He attempted to dismiss the suggestion that Lipski had entered Mrs Angel's room with an immoral purpose, to which Mr Justice Stephen interjected again, observing that the prosecution 'had not given up the motive of immorality.' McIntyre contended that he believed the fact the accused was found under the bed was far more in keeping with his statement that he was attacked by two men and concluded that the evidence for the Crown 'was too inconclusive to justify the jury in finding the prisoner guilty upon a charge of this awfully serious character.'

In his lengthy summing up, Mr Justice Stephen pointed out the lack of motive for robbery and went so far as to state that:

> It was more probable that passion was the motive for the crime, and that if that were so it would rather be the act of one man than two. It was shown that the prisoner had not been acquainted with the deceased and her husband, and consequently if it was the prisoner who committed the act it must have been under the influence of a sudden temptation.

But he did go on to point out: 'The prisoner was a man of good character and was engaged to be married, and these were circumstances which the jury should take into consideration in favour of the prisoner.' Mr Justice Stephen's final directions to the jury asked them to consider:

> One could hardly imagine that two men who were strangers to each other should walk down from the workshop and go into the deceased's room for the purpose of committing an assault upon her, and it was almost as difficult to imagine that they should go into the room of a woman as poor as themselves for the purpose of taking a few clothes, which after all they did not take, and why should they rob the prisoner? How could they reconcile the prisoner's statement with the fact that the door was locked on the inside? The locking of the door was a circumstance of great importance supposing the jury were of opinion that it was locked. The observations made on the part of the defence as to the improbability of the prisoner having committed the crime were of very great importance, and should be carefully considered by the jury. If the jury came to the conclusion that the prisoner was the person who committed the offence, then the natural inference was that he attempted to commit suicide afterwards.

The jury retired at 4.43 p.m. and just eight minutes later they returned a verdict of guilty as charged against Israel Lipski. Asked if he had anything to say, he replied in Yiddish, 'I did not do it.' Lipski outwardly remained composed as Mr Justice Stephen donned the black cap and pronounced the death sentence upon him. Lipski was then 'taken down' and removed to Newgate to await his execution.

After the trial questions were raised about the interventions and weak cross-examination from the counsel for the defence. Lipski's solicitor, Mr John Hayward, had found what he believed to be great weaknesses in the evidence presented by the prosecution, and even believed he had found a witness who would state another man bought some nitric acid from another shop at the time of the crime: this man also

Sketches of counsel, witnesses and the accused (centre) in the Lipski trial.

claimed to be a stick maker, but did not resemble Lipski. Hayward sent telegrams to senior government officials, placed adverts in national papers and even produced a pamphlet detailing the 'evidence', and as a result a question was asked in the House of Commons. *The Times* of 15 August 1887 reported:

Strenuous efforts were made on Saturday afternoon to obtain from the Home Secretary a reprieve of Lipski. Directly after Mr Matthews's reply in the House of Commons to Mr Graham, Mr L.J. Greenberg, who has been assisting Mr Hayward in his endeavours to obtain a respite of the sentence, called at the House and saw Baron de Worms, with whom Mr Greenberg had a prolonged interview. Baron H. de Worms advised Mr Greenberg to make his statement to the Home Office, and this was done. Subsequently Mr Hayward and his managing clerk, together with Mr Greenberg, proceeded to the House of Commons, where they were met by Baron Henry de Worms, Sir Wilfred Lawson, Mr Hanbury, Mr Graham, and others, and by them introduced to the Home Secretary in his private rooms. With the Home Secretary were Sir Henry James and Mr Lushington. The interview lasted upwards of an hour and a half. The Home Secretary assured the deputation that, as he had promised in the House, he would keep his mind open to the last moment and would not allow the law to take its course if he saw the slightest grounds for altering his decision. During the interview Mr Hayward received from the Home Secretary an acknowledgement in behalf of Her Majesty of the telegram that had been despatched to Osborne.

Campaigning editor W.T. Stead:
'Lipski must not be hanged.'

Extended media interest came from mostly Jewish newspapers, with the notable exception of the *Pall Mall Gazette* which took on the campaign for a reprieve in an article written by its campaigning editor W.T. Stead, heralded with the sensational statement: 'Lipski must not be hanged. Why not? – For a very simple but very sufficient reason. Mr Justice Stephen, who tried Lipski, and whose summing up contributed not a little to his conviction, has since been converted, and is aghast at the prospect of hanging a possibly innocent man.' Justice Stephen's response, published in *The Times*, spoke first of a breach of confidence and then used terms such as 'it was absolutely false and unfounded' as he dealt with the most contentious elements of the article.

However, any criticism of the case or claims of 'new evidence' – or any suggestion that an innocent man may be sent to the gallows – soon became academic: after all appeals were lodged, and all avenues exhausted, and it was certain there was to be no reprieve, Lipski confessed. He exonerated all those he had implicated in the crime.

What follows is a transcription of Lipski's confession. I leave it to the judgement of the reader to decide how believable his sworn 'whole truth' really was, especially if one recalls the witness statements of those who discovered the body of Miriam Angel at 16 Batty Street on the morning of Tuesday 28 June 1887:

> I Israel Lipski, before I appear before God in judgement, desire to speak the whole truth concerning the crime of which I am accused. I will not die with a lie on my lips. I will not let others suffer, even on suspicion, for my sin. I alone was guilty of the murder of

Miriam Angel. I thought the woman had money in her room, so I entered – the door being unlocked and the woman asleep. I had no thought of violating her, and I swear I never approached her with that object, nor did I wrong her in this way.

Miriam Angel awoke before I could search about for money, and cried out, but very softly. Thereupon I struck her on the head, and seized her by the neck, and closed her mouth with my hand, so that she would not arouse the attention of those who were about the house. I had long been tired of life, and had bought a pennyworth of aquafortis that morning for putting an end to my life. Suddenly I thought of the bottle I had in my pocket, and drew it out and poured some of the contents down her throat. She fainted, and, recognising my desperate condition, I took the rest. The bottle was an old one which I had formerly used, and was the same as that which I had taken with me to the oil shop. The quantity of aquafortis I took had no effect on me.

Hearing the voices of people coming upstairs I crawled under the bed. The woman seemed already dead. There was only a very short time of my entering the room until I was taken away. In the agitation I also fainted. I don't know how it was that my arms became abraded. I did not feel it, and was not aware of it.

As to the door being locked from the inside, I myself did this immediately after I entered the room, wishing not to be interrupted. I solemnly declare that Rosenbloom and Schmuss know nothing whatever of the crime of which I have been guilty, and I alone. I implore them to pardon me for having in my despair tried to cast the blame upon them. I also beseech the forgiveness of the bereaved husband. I admit that I have had a fair trial, and acknowledge the justice of the sentence that has been passed upon me.

I desire to thank Mr Hayward for his efforts on my behalf, as well as all those who have interested themselves in me during this unhappy time. This confession is made of my own free will and is written down by Mr Singer at my request. May God comfort my loving father and mother, and may he accept my repentance and my death as an atonement for all my sins.

Dated Sunday, Aug. 21 1887

Signed: Israel Lipski

Witnesses: S. Singer, Minister

E.S. Milman, Governor of Her Majesty's Prison, Newgate

After Lipski had dictated his confession in Yiddish, Rabbi Simeon Singer asked Lipski if he wished to write to his parents in Warsaw, and this he dictated in his native language. He also sorrowfully directed that another letter should be sent to Mrs Lyons, the mother of his fiancée. Having unburdened himself and now facing the gallows, Lipski was conscious all his affairs should be in order and asked the minister to pay a 'trifling debt' he owed to a fellow lodger, and that his effects and stock be sold to reimburse his landlady.

On the morning of his execution Lipski rose shortly after 5 a.m., and by 6 a.m. Rabbi Singer was in attendance again, and remained with him in prayer for nearly two hours. The *Penny Illustrated Paper* evocatively recorded the last moments of Israel Lipski thus:

The Newgate gallows.

Executioner James Berry.

Two or three minutes before eight o'clock the representatives of the press, eight in number, were admitted to the yard in which stands the scaffold, and simultaneously a procession consisting of the Sheriffs, Under Sheriff, the Governor of the prison, the surgeons, the condemned man, Mr Singer, and some officials, in addition to Berry, the executioner, started from the condemned cell, in which the preliminary pinioning process had been performed without any demur on the part of Lipski, after he had expressed his gratitude to Mr Singer and the officials for the kindness extended to him.

Before he took his stand on the scaffold, an interpreter was called forward and by request of the Sheriffs asked Lipski if he had anything to say. The reply, delivered in a low tone of voice, was brief, 'I have no more to say; I am guilty.' While the last preparations were being made, Lipski was repeating the responses in a moaning voice; then Berry disappeared, the drop fell, and death was apparently instantaneous. The black flag was hoisted over the prison, which, it is said, was the signal for a loud cheer from the mob outside the gates, just as the Minister was reciting in trembling tones the final prayer.

In his memoirs, James Berry, Lipski's executioner, recalled:

At Lipski's execution the crowd was the largest I have ever seen, many of the people remained hanging about for hours. The excitement was intense, but there was no sympathy for the prisoner. There were many Jews in the crowd, and wherever they were noticed they were hustled and kicked about, and insulted in every imaginable manner; for the hatred displayed by the mob was extended from Lipski to his race. When the black flag was hoisted it was received with three ringing cheers. Altogether, the crowd showed the utmost detestation of the murderer.

As per the full sentence of the law, Lipski's body was placed in a grave and covered in quicklime within the walls of the prison, but his name lived on for years as a colloquial term of derision and abuse, often aimed against members of the Jewish population in the East End.

4

THE AUTUMN OF TERROR

Jack the Ripper, 1888

In the long catalogue of crimes which has been compiled in our modern days there is nothing to be found, perhaps, which has so darkened the horizon of humanity and shadowed the vista of man's better nature as the series of mysterious murders committed in Whitechapel during the latter part of the year 1888. From east to west, from north to south the horror ran throughout the land. Men spoke of it with bated breath, and pale-lipped, shuddered as they read the dreadful details. A lurid pall rested over that densely populated district of London, and people, looking at it afar off, smelt blood. The superstitious said the skies had been of deeper red that autumn, presaging desperate and direful deeds, and aliens of the neighbourhood, filled with strange phantasies brought from foreign shores, whispered that evil spirits were abroad.

So wrote Harold Furniss in his introduction to the Jack the Ripper editions of his *Famous Crimes Magazine* in the early years of the twentieth century. After the terror whipped up by the media frenzy and lurid illustrations of the crimes committed by the Whitechapel Fiend, later known as Jack the Ripper, the mystery and horror of the crimes has lingered on, permeating the social 'memory' or folklore of British society, as one generation after another is chilled by the faceless, top-hatted gentleman murderer, who strode the mean streets of the East End of London in search of another victim. That's the myth... or is it? That's the fascination of 'hunting' Jack the Ripper; for 120 years new theories naming suspects from the humblest to the highest in the land have argued, counter argued, named, shamed, and even fabricated evidence of who Jack the Ripper really was. I do not think it will now ever be possible to conclusively prove who he was – certainly not so a court would be convinced – but that does not mean we will ever stop hunting for him.

In this chapter I will examine the 'canonical five' murders widely agreed by crime historians and many Ripperologists as being perpetrated by Jack the Ripper.

Let us primarily concern ourselves with the salient points of fact about the murders. For the purposes of this exercise, we shall predominantly use official records and newspaper articles, where we can read the accounts of contemporary witnesses to the discovery of the bodies, the statements of the doctors who examined the victims, and read of the subsequent police investigations carried out at the time.

We begin on the evening of 30 August 1888, which was no ordinary evening in the East End. The night was interspersed with heavy downpours of rain accompanied by rolls of thunder and flashes of lightning; the sky turning an ominous shade of red caused by two dock fires and the accompanying pall of smoke. The *East London Advertiser* described it thus:

> The scene at half-past 10 was an imposing one. In the enormous docks, crammed with goods of incalculable value, with vast buildings on every side, and with great vessels in the wet docks, firemen, policemen and dock officers were either watching or aiding in endeavouring to extinguish the fire, while an enormous crowd gathered round the great gates and gazed at the progress of the fire from a distance. In a great shed building close to the fire the steamers had been drawn up in little clusters of twos and threes, and were pumping continuously with a deafening noise, while the horses, which had been unharnessed, stood quietly in couples in every corner. The water poured over the granite stones of the docks in torrents, and the whole scene was brilliantly illuminated by the fire above.

It was hardly surprising the East End streets were abuzz with people talking about and going to see the fire at the Shadwell Dry Dock.

Mary Ann Nichols was on the Whitechapel Road, probably soliciting. She was 42 years old and had been married, but it had proved to be a turbulent union, and after a number of separations Mary finally walked out on her husband and children in 1881. There then began a tragic and all-too-typical tale: Mary's life descended further and further into an abyss of drink, destitution, prostitution, sleeping on the streets and in dosshouses, and living from workhouse to workhouse. In August 1888 her sole source of income was from prostitution. Mary, now known to many on the streets as 'Polly', had been living in a room she shared with four other women in a dosshouse at 18 Thrawl Street, but had recently moved to another, known as the White House at 56 Flower and Dean Street, where men were allowed to share a bed with a woman. In 1883 Flower and Dean Street had been described as 'perhaps the foulest and most dangerous street in the whole metropolis' (nothing had changed by 1888) and, along with nearby Thrawl Street, made up part of the area of Spitalfields known as the 'evil quarter mile.'

At 12.30 a.m. on 31 August 1888, Polly, who had been drinking at the Frying Pan public house on the corner of Brick Lane and Thrawl Street, was on her way back to her old lodging house at 18 Thrawl Street. After about an hour there, Polly was turned away by the deputy because she did not have the 4*d* required to stay the night. She was described as being 'worse for drink, but not drunk'. After telling the deputy to save her a bed, she turned to the lodging house door, laughing, 'I'll soon get my doss money; see what a jolly bonnet I've got now.' She indicated the bonnet she was wearing (which the lodging-house deputy had not seen before).

Polly was next encountered by her old room-mate, Emily Holland, outside a grocer's shop on the corner of Whitechapel Road and Osborn Street and nearly opposite the parish church, where the clock had just struck 2.30 a.m. Emily had been watching the Shadwell Dry Dock fire. Polly was, by then, much the worse for drink and was staggering against the wall. Emily tried to persuade her to come home with her, but Polly declined, telling Emily that she had had her doss money three times that day and had drunk it away, and declaring confidently, 'It won't be long before I'm back.' Emily could only watch as Polly staggered off eastward down Whitechapel Road.

Less than an hour and a quarter later, and just under three-quarters of a mile away, Polly's mutilated body was discovered on Buck's Row, in a location opposite the Essex Wharf warehouse, Brown and Eagle Wool warehouse and Schneiders Cap factory – in the gateway entrance to an old stable yard between a board school and a row of terraced cottages. Her body lay face up with her head almost underneath the window of the end terrace house (known as the 'New Cottage') next to the stable-yard gates. This was the home of a widow named Mrs Green, who lived there with two sons, and a daughter who shared her bedroom with her. Despite claiming to be a light sleeper, neither Mrs Green nor any of her family claimed to have heard a thing until the police arrived.

The body was discovered by Charles Andrew Cross, who was on his way to work as a carman for Messrs Pickford & Co. (a job he had served for over twenty years). At the inquest, which was held on Saturday 1 September 1888 at the Working Lads' Institute on Whitechapel Road before Mr Wynne E. Baxter, the coroner for South-East Middlesex, Cross gave the following account:

[At] about half-past three on Friday I left my home go to work, as I passed through Buck's-row I saw on the opposite side something lying against the gateway, but I couldn't make out what it was. I thought it was a tarpaulin sheet. I walked into the middle of the road, and saw that it was the figure of a woman. I then heard the footsteps of a man [another carman named Robert Paul] going up Buck's-row, about 40 yards away, in the direction I had just come from. When he came up I said to him, 'Come and look over here; there is a woman lying on the pavement.' We crossed over to the body, and I took hold of the woman's hands, which were cold and limp. I said, 'I believe she is dead.' I touched her face, which felt warm. The other man, placing his hand on her heart, said 'I think she is breathing, but very little if she is.' I suggested we should give her a prop, but my companion refused to touch her... I didn't notice that her throat was cut, the night being very dark. We left the deceased, and in Baker's-row we met PC Mizen, who we told we had seen a woman lying in Buck's-row, I said, 'She looks to me to be either dead or drunk; but for my part I think she is dead.' The policeman said, 'All right,' and then walked on. The other man left me soon after.

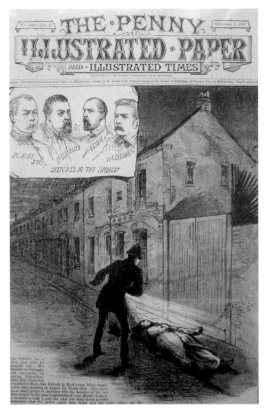

Cover story: PC John Neil 97J shines his lamp on the body of Polly Nichols on Buck's Row. (*Stewart P. Evans*)

Mr Baxter enquired further:

Baxter: Did you know the other man?

Cross: I had never seen him before.

Baxter: Did you see anyone else in Buck's Row?

Cross: No, there was nobody there when he and the other man left.

Baxter: And the woman on the ground, could you see no injuries at all?

Cross: In my opinion she looked as if she had been outraged and gone off in a swoon; but I had no idea that there were any serious injuries.

At the same time that Cross and Paul encountered Constable Mizen, PC John Neil 97J was on patrol in Buck's Row. His statement at the inquest was as follows:

Yesterday morning I was proceeding down Buck's-row, Whitechapel, going towards Brady-street. There was not a soul about. I had been round there half an hour previously, and I saw no one then. I was on the right-hand side of the street, when I noticed a figure lying in the street. It was dark at the time, though there was a street lamp shining at the end of the row. I went across and found deceased lying outside a gateway, her head towards the east. The gateway was closed. It was about 9ft or 10ft high, and led to some stables. There were houses from the gateway eastward, and the School Board school occupies the westward. On the opposite side of the road is Essex Wharf. Deceased was lying lengthways along the street, her left hand touching the gate. I examined the body by the aid of my lamp, and noticed blood oozing from a wound in the throat. She was lying on her back, with her clothes disarranged. I felt her arm, which was quite warm from the joints upwards. Her eyes were wide open. Her bonnet was off and lying at her side, close to the left hand. I heard a constable passing Brady-street, so I called him. I did not whistle. I said to him, 'Run at once for Dr Llewellyn,' and, seeing another constable in Baker's-row, I sent him for the ambulance. The doctor arrived in a very short time. I had, in the meantime, rung the bell at Essex Wharf, and asked if any disturbance had been heard. The reply was 'No.' Sergeant Kirby came after, and he knocked. The doctor looked at the woman and then said, 'Move her to the mortuary. She is dead, and I will make a further examination of her.' We placed her on the ambulance, and moved her there.

Inspector Spratling came to the mortuary, and while taking a description of the deceased turned up her clothes, and found that she was disembowelled. This had not been noticed by any of them before. On the body was found a piece of comb and a bit of looking-glass. No money was found, but an unmarked white handkerchief was found in her pocket.

Baxter: Did you notice any blood where she was found?

PC Neil: There was a pool of blood just where her neck was lying. It was running from the wound in her neck.

Baxter: Did you hear any noise that night?

PC Neil: No; I heard nothing. The farthest I had been that night was just through the Whitechapel-road and up Baker's-row. I was never far away from the spot.

Baxter: Whitechapel-road is busy in the early morning, I believe. Could anybody have escaped that way?

PC Neil: Oh yes, sir. I saw a number of women in the main road going home. At that time anyone could have got away.

Baxter: Someone searched the ground, I believe?

PC Neil: Yes; I examined it while the doctor was being sent for.

Inspector Spratling: I examined the road, sir, in daylight.

Baxter (to *PC Neil*): Did you see a trap in the road at all?

PC Neil: No.

Baxter: Knowing that the body was warm, did it not strike you that it might just have been laid there, and that the woman was killed elsewhere?

PC Neil: I examined the road, but did not see the mark of wheels. The first to arrive on the scene after I had discovered the body were two men who work at a slaughterhouse opposite. They said they knew nothing of the affair, and that they had not heard any screams. I had previously seen the men at work. That would be about a quarter-past three, or half an hour before I found the body.

Dr Rees Ralph Llewellyn was then called to give evidence.

On Friday morning I was called to Buck's-row about four o'clock. The constable told me what I was wanted for. On reaching Buck's Row I found the deceased woman lying flat on her back in the pathway, her legs extended. I found she was dead, and that she had severe injuries to her throat. Her hands and wrists were cold, but the body and lower extremities were warm. I examined her chest and felt the heart. It was dark at the time. I believe she had not been dead more than half-an-hour. I am quite certain that the injuries to her neck were not self-inflicted. There was very little blood round the neck. There were no marks of any struggle or of blood, as if the body had been dragged. I told the police to take her to the mortuary, and I would make another examination. About an hour later I was sent for by the Inspector to see the injuries he had discovered on the body. I went, and saw that the abdomen was cut very extensively. I have this morning made a post-mortem examination of the body. I found it to be that of a female about forty or forty-five years. Five of the teeth are missing, and there is a slight laceration of the tongue. On the right side of the face there is a bruise running along the lower part of the jaw. It might have been caused by a blow with the fist or pressure by the thumb. On the left side of the face there was a circular bruise, which also might have been done by the pressure of the fingers. On the left side of the neck, about an inch below the jaw, there was an incision about 4in long and running from a point immediately below the ear. An inch below on the same side, and commencing about an inch in front of it, was a circular incision terminating at a point about 3in below the right jaw. This incision completely severs all the tissues down to the vertebrae. The large vessels of the neck on both sides were severed. The incision is about 8in long. These cuts must have been caused with a long-bladed knife, moderately sharp, and used with great violence. No blood at all was found on the breast either of the body or clothes. There were no injuries about the body till just about the lower part of the abdomen. Two or 3in from the left side was a wound running in a jagged manner. It was a very deep wound, and the tissues were cut through. There were several incisions running across the abdomen. On the right side there were also three or four similar cuts running downwards. All these had been caused by a knife, which had been used violently and been used downwards. The wounds were from left to right, and might have been done by a left-handed person. All the injuries had been done by the same instrument.

Press reports rapidly drew together a number of previously unconnected murders in the East End and soon headlines were announcing that Polly Nichols was another victim of the killer they dubbed 'The Whitechapel Murderer' or 'Fiend'. Among them was an Elizabeth Smith, Martha Tabram and even an unnamed (and probably fictional) woman who was allegedly murdered during Christmas week in 1887.

The press announced the police were questioning slaughtermen. Boot finisher John Pizer, a man known in the Whitechapel area as 'Leather Apron' was wanted for questioning in connection with murders because of his reputation for 'ill-using prostitutes.' A Polish Jew, Pizer – who gained his nickname because of his habit of wearing his work apron on the street – was well known to locals and to the police. On 10 September 1888 Pizer was arrested by Sergeant Thick and several sharp, long-bladed knives were found on his premises at 22 Mulberry Street – but that is hardly

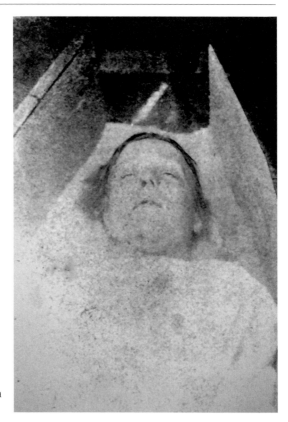

Mortuary photograph of Mary Ann 'Polly' Nichols. (*Stewart P. Evans*)

One of the sightings of a Jack the Ripper suspect depicted in *The Illustrated Police News*, shortly after the 'Hanbury Street Horror' murder of Annie Chapman.

surprising, as his trade involved the use of such tools. Pizer was taken to Leman Street police station: fearing for his life, his friends joined him, confirmed his alibi and he was released the following day. However, the broadsheets still demanded the capture of 'Leather Apron' – no longer a name just for Pizer but a generic term for the Whitechapel Murderer, thought to be a slaughterman or tradesman skilled with his knife (such as a cork worker or cobbler). But we must not get ahead of ourselves, because by the time Pizer had been arrested, there had already been another murder.

Annie Chapman was 47. She had once enjoyed a good standard of living, was married and had three children, but, as ever, it seems the 'demon drink' claimed another family and she and her husband separated under claims she led a drunken and immoral lifestyle. Her husband was known as a heavy drinker too. John Chapman supported his wife with regular payments of 10s a week, but these stopped when he died on Christmas Day 1886. Up to that time Annie had been living with another man, but he too left her – probably because the regular money dried up. Annie was then left to fend for herself, but despite having another relationship she had no means of earning, so she turned to prostitution and regularly resided at 'Crossingham's', a lodging house catering for about 300 people at 35 Dorset Street, Spitalfields.

At 1.35 a.m. on Saturday 8 September 1888 Annie arrived at Crossingham's. She had been in and out of the lodging house a number of times during the evening, and was sporting a black eye after a fight with another woman a few days earlier. She had been drinking and was eating a baked potato. John 'Brummy' Evans, the lodging house's elderly nightwatchman, was sent to collect her bed money but she went upstairs to see Timothy Donovan, the deputy in charge, in his office. Annie told him, 'I haven't sufficient money for my bed, but don't let it. I shall not be long before I'm in.' Donovan chastised her, saying, 'You can find money for your beer and you can't find money for your bed.' Nonplussed, Annie stood in the doorway for two or three minutes before adding, 'Never mind, Tim, I'll soon be back.' She left peaceably. Donovan later recalled, 'She walked straight. Generally on Saturdays she was the worse for drink.' As Annie left she saw Watchman Evans again and said, 'I won't be long, Brummy. See that Tim keeps the bed for me.' Evans watched her leave and enter Little Paternoster Row, heading in the direction of Brushfield Street; he finally lost sight of her as she turned towards Spitalfields Market.

The last witness to see Annie alive was Mrs Elizabeth Long, who passed her when she was a few yards from 29 Hanbury Street. On the fourth day of the inquest before the coroner, Mr Wynne Baxter, on Wednesday 19 September 1888, she stated:

On Saturday 8 September, about half past five o'clock in the morning, I was passing down Hanbury Street, from home, on my way to Spitalfields Market. I knew the time, because I heard the brewer's clock strike half-past five just before I got to the street. I passed 29 Hanbury Street. On the right-hand side, the same side as the house, I saw a man and a woman standing on the pavement talking. The man's back was turned towards Brick Lane, and the woman's was towards the market. They were standing only a few yards nearer Brick Lane from 29 Hanbury Street. I saw the woman's face.

Street of infamy: Dorset Street.

Have seen the deceased in the mortuary, and I am sure the woman that I saw in Hanbury Street was the deceased. I did not see the man's face, but I noticed that he was dark. He was wearing a brown low-crowned felt hat. I think he had on a dark coat, though I am not certain. By the look of him he seemed to me a man over forty years of age. He appeared to me to be a little taller than the deceased.

Baxter: Did he look like a working man, or what?
Long: He looked like a foreigner.
Baxter: Did he look like a dock labourer, or a workman, or what?
Long: I should say he looked like what I should call shabby-genteel.
Baxter: Were they talking loudly?
Long: They were talking pretty loudly. I overheard him say to her 'Will you?' and she replied, 'Yes.' That is all I heard, and I heard this as I passed. I left them standing there, and I did not look back, so I cannot say where they went to.

The body of Annie Chapman was discovered in the early hours of Thursday 26 September 1888, in the back yard of 29 Hanbury Street, Spitalfields.

On Monday 10 September 1888, at the Working Lads' Institute on Whitechapel Road, Mr Wynne Baxter opened the inquest into the death of Annie Chapman. The jury viewed the corpse at the mortuary in Montague Street, but all evidences of the outrage to which the deceased had been subjected were concealed. The clothing was also inspected. These and a few tragic effects were listed as:

- A long black-figured coat that came down to her knees
- A black skirt
- Brown bodice
- Another bodice
- Two petticoats
- A large pocket worn under the skirt and tied about the waist with strings (empty when found)
- Lace-up boots
- Red and white striped woollen stockings
- Neckerchief, white with a wide red border
- Scrap of muslin
- One small tooth comb
- One comb in a paper case
- Scrap of envelope containing two pills bearing the seal of the Sussex Regiment postmarked 'London, 28, Aug., 1888' inscribed is a partial address consisting of the letter M, the number 2 as if the beginning of an address and an S
- Curiously, Annie was known to have worn two brass rings on her middle finger: these were missing after her murder

The circumstances of the discovery of Annie's body were given by John Davies, who was employed as a carman at Leadenhall Market:

> I have lodged at 29 Hanbury-street for a fortnight, and I occupied the top front room on the third floor with my wife and three sons, who live with me. On Friday night I went to bed at eight o'clock, and my wife followed about half an hour later. My sons came to bed at different times, the last one at about a quarter to eleven. There is a weaving shed window, or light across the room. It was not open during the night. I was awake from 3 a.m. to 5 a.m. on Saturday, and then fell asleep until a quarter to six, when the clock at Spitalfields Church struck. I had a cup of tea and went downstairs to the back yard. The house faces Hanbury Street, with one window on the ground floor and a front door at the side leading into a passage which runs through into the yard. There is a back door at the end of this passage opening into the yard. Neither of the doors was able to be locked, and I have never seen them locked. Anyone who knows where the latch of the front door is could open it and go along the passage into the back yard.

Baxter: When you went into the yard on Saturday morning was the yard door open or shut?

Davies: I found it shut. I cannot say whether it was latched – I can't remember. I have been too much upset. The front street door was wide open and thrown against the wall. I was not surprised to find the front door open, as it was not unusual. I opened the back door, and stood in the entrance.

Baxter: Will you describe the yard?

Davies: It is a large yard. Facing the door, on the opposite side, on my left as I was standing, there is a shed, in which Mrs Richardson keeps her wood. In the right-hand corner there is a closet. The yard is separated from the next premises on both sides by close wooden fencing, about 5ft 6in high. From the steps to the fence is about 3ft. There are three stone steps, unprotected, leading from the door to the yard, which is at a lower level than that of the passage. Directly I opened the door I saw a woman lying down in the left-hand recess, between the stone steps and the fence. She was on her back, with her head towards the house and her legs towards the wood shed. The clothes were up to her groins. I did not go into the yard, but left the house by the front door, and called the attention of two men to the circumstances. They work at Mr Bailey's, a packing-case maker, of Hanbury Street. I do not know their names, but I know them by sight. Mr Bailey's is three doors off 29, Hanbury Street, on the same side of the road. The two men were waiting outside the workshop. They came into the passage, and saw the sight. They did not go into the yard, but ran to find a policeman. We all came out of the house together. I went to the Commercial Street police station to report the case. No one in the house was informed by me of what I had discovered. I told the inspector at the police-station, and after a while I returned to Hanbury Street, but did not re-enter the house. As I passed I saw constables there.

Baxter: Have you ever seen the deceased before?

Davies: No.

Baxter: Have you ever seen women in the passage?

Davies: Mrs Richardson has said there have been. I have not seen them myself. I have only been in the house a fortnight.

Baxter: Did you hear any noise that Saturday morning?

Davies: No, sir.

Davies was also asked if he was the first person up on the morning in question: he was not, and stated there was a lodger named Thompson, who was called at half-past three. However, Thompson had not seen or heard anything untoward; neither had John Richardson, of John Street, Spitalfields, a market porter who assisted his mother in her packing-crate business at 29 Hanbury Street. He had gone to 29 Hanbury Street between 4.45 a.m. and 4.50 a.m. to check the cellar was secure as a matter of routine after they had suffered a robbery where some tools had been taken from the cellar.

Baxter: Was the front door open?

Richardson: No, it was closed. I lifted the latch and went through the passage to the yard door.

Baxter: Did you go into the yard?

Richardson: No, the yard door was shut. I opened it and sat on the doorstep, and cut a piece of leather off my boot with an old table-knife, about 5in long. I kept the knife upstairs at John Street. I had been feeding a rabbit with a carrot that I had cut up, and I put the knife in my pocket. I do not usually carry it there. After cutting the leather off

Cover of *The Illustrated Police News*, September 22 1888, depicting the story of the murder of Annie Chapman – 'The Hanbury Street Horror'.

my boot I tied my boot up, and went out of the house into the market. I did not close the back door. It closed itself. I shut the front door.

Baxter: How long were you there?

Richardson: About two minutes at most.

Baxter: Was it light?

Richardson: It was getting light, but I could see all over the place.

Baxter: Did you notice whether there was any object outside?

Richardson: I could not have failed to notice the deceased had she been lying there then. I saw the body two or three minutes before the doctor came. I was then in the adjoining yard. Thomas Pierman had told me about the murder in the market. When I was on the doorstep I saw that the padlock on the cellar door was in its proper place.

Baxter: Did you sit on the top step?

Richardson: No, on the middle step; my feet were on the flags of the yard.

Baxter: You must have been quite close to where the deceased was found?

Richardson: Yes, I must have seen her if she had been there.

Baxter: You have been there at all hours of the night?

Richardson: Yes.

Baxter: Have you ever seen any strangers there?

Richardson: Yes, plenty, at all hours – both men and women. I have often turned them
   out. We have had them on our first floor as well, on the landing.

Baxter: Do you mean to say that they go there for an immoral purpose?

Richardson: Yes, they do.

Once news got out of another 'East End Horror' crowds came to view the body and
site of the killing; local residents charged a penny to anyone wishing look out of the
windows of adjoining properties to views the back yard murder scene. But no one
could have anticipated the comments delivered later in the proceedings when Mr
George Baxter Phillips, divisional surgeon of police, gave his evidence.

On Saturday last I was called by the police at 6.20 a.m. to 29 Hanbury Street, and arrived
at half-past six. I found the body of the deceased lying in the yard on her back, on the
left hand of the steps that lead from the passage. The head was about 6in in front of the
level of the bottom step, and the feet were towards a shed at the end of the yard. The
left arm was across the left breast, and the legs were drawn up, the feet resting on the
ground, and the knees turned outwards. The face was swollen and turned on the right
side, and the tongue protruded between the front teeth, but not beyond the lips; it was
much swollen. The small intestines and other portions were lying on the right side of the
body on the ground above the right shoulder, but attached. There was a large quantity
of blood, with a part of the stomach above the left shoulder. I searched the yard and
found a small piece of coarse muslin, a small-tooth comb, and a pocket-comb, in a paper
case, near the railing. They had apparently been arranged there. I also discovered various
other articles, which I handed to the police. The body was cold, except that there was
a certain remaining heat, under the intestines, in the body. Stiffness of the limbs was
not marked, but it was commencing. The throat was disseevered deeply. I noticed that
the incision of the skin was jagged, and reached right round the neck. On the back wall
of the house, between the steps and the palings, on the left side, about 18in from the
ground, there were about six patches of blood, varying in size from a sixpenny piece to
a small point, and on the wooden fence there were smears of blood, corresponding to
where the head of the deceased laid, and immediately above the part where the blood had
mainly flowed from the neck, which was well clotted. Having received instructions soon
after two o'clock on Saturday afternoon, I went to the labour-yard of the Whitechapel
Union for the purpose of further examining the body and making the usual post-mortem
investigation. I was surprised to find that the body had been stripped and was laying
ready on the table. It was under great disadvantage I made my examination. As on many
occasions I have met with the same difficulty, I now raise my protest, as I have before,
that members of my profession should be called upon to perform their duties under these
inadequate circumstances.

Baxter: The mortuary is not fitted for a post-mortem examination. It is only a shed.
   There is no adequate convenience, and nothing fit, and at certain seasons of the year it
   is dangerous to the operator. As a matter of fact there is no public mortuary from the

City of London up to Bow. There is one at Mile End, but it belongs to the workhouse, and is not used for general purposes.

Phillips: The body had been attended to since its removal to the mortuary, and probably partially washed. I noticed a bruise over the right temple. There was a bruise under the clavicle, and there were two distinct bruises, each the size of a man's thumb, on the fore part of the chest. The stiffness of the limbs was then well-marked. The finger nails were turgid. There was an old scar of long standing on the left of the frontal bone. On the left side the stiffness was more noticeable, and especially in the fingers, which were partly closed. There was an abrasion over the bend of the first joint of the ring finger, and there were distinct markings of a ring or rings – probably the latter. There were small sores on the fingers. The throat had been severed. The incisions of the skin indicated that they had been made from the left side of the neck on a line with the angle of the jaw, carried entirely round and again in front of the neck, and ending at a point about midway between the jaw and the sternum or breast bone on the right hand. There were two distinct clean cuts on the body of the vertebrae on the left side of the spine. They were parallel to each other, and separated by about half an inch. The muscular structures between the side processes of bone of the vertebrae had an appearance as if an attempt had been made to separate the bones of the neck. There are various other mutilations of the body, but I am of opinion that they occurred subsequently to the death of the woman and to the large escape of blood from the neck. [The witness pauses.] I am entirely in your hands, sir, but is it necessary that I should describe the further mutilations? From what I have said I can state the cause of death.

Baxter: The object of the inquiry is not only to ascertain the cause of death, but the means by which it occurred. Any mutilation which took place afterwards may suggest the character of the man who did it. Possibly you can give us the conclusions to which you have come respecting the instrument used?

Phillips: You don't wish for details. I think if it is possible to escape the details it would be advisable. The cause of death is visible from the injuries I have described.

Baxter: You have kept a record of them?

Phillips: I have.

Baxter: Supposing anyone is charged with the offence, they would have to come out then, and it might be a matter of comment that the same evidence was not given at the inquest.

Phillips: I am entirely in your hands.

Baxter: We will postpone that for the present. You can give your opinion as to how the death was caused.

Phillips: From these appearances I am of the opinion that the breathing was interfered with previous to death, and that death arose from syncope, or failure of the heart's action, in consequence of the loss of blood caused by the severance of the throat.

Baxter: Was the instrument used at the throat the same as that used at the abdomen?

Phillips: Very probably. It must have been a very sharp knife, probably with a thin, narrow blade, and at least 6 to 8in in length, and perhaps longer.

Baxter: Is it possible that any instrument used by a military man, such as a bayonet, would have done it?

Phillips: No, it would not be a bayonet.

Baxter: Would it have been such an instrument as a medical man uses for post-mortem examinations?

Phillips: The ordinary post-mortem case perhaps does not contain such a weapon.

Baxter: Would any instrument that slaughterers employ have caused the injuries?

Phillips: Yes, well ground down.

Baxter: Would the knife of a cobbler or of any person in the leather trades have done?

Phillips: I think the knife used in those trades would not be long enough in the blade.

Baxter: Was there any anatomical knowledge displayed?

Phillips: I think there was. There were indications of it. My own impression is that the anatomical knowledge was only less displayed or indicated in consequence of haste. The person evidently was hindered from making a more complete dissection in consequence of the haste.

Baxter: Was the whole of the body there?

Phillips: No, the absent portions being from the abdomen.

Baxter: Are those portions such as would require anatomical knowledge to extract?

Phillips: I think the mode in which they were extracted did show some anatomical knowledge.

Baxter: You do not think they could have been lost accidentally in the transit of the body to the mortuary?

Phillips: I was not present at the transit. I carefully closed up the clothes of the woman. Some portions had been excised.

Baxter: How long had the deceased been dead when you saw her?

Phillips: I should say at least two hours, and probably more; but it is right to say that it was a fairly cold morning, and that the body would be more apt to cool rapidly from its having lost the greater portion of its blood.

Baxter: Was there any evidence of any struggle?

Phillips: No, not about the body of the woman. You do not forget the smearing of blood about the palings.

Baxter: In your opinion did she enter the yard alive?

Phillips: I am positive of it. I made a thorough search of the passage, and I saw no trace of blood, which must have been visible had she been taken into the yard.

In his summing up, Baxter added some revelations of his own:

The object of the murderer appears palpably shown by the facts, and it is not necessary to assume lunacy, for it is clear that there is a market for the object of the murder. To show you this, I must mention a fact which at the same time proves the assistance which publicity and the newspaper press afford in the detection of crime. Within a few hours of the issue of the morning papers containing a report of the medical evidence given at the last sitting of the Court, I received a communication from an officer of one

Mortuary photograph of Annie
Chapman. (*Stewart P. Evans*)

of our great medical schools, that they had information which might or might not have
a distinct bearing on our inquiry. I attended at the first opportunity, and was told by the
sub-curator of the Pathological Museum that some months ago an American had called
on him, and asked him to procure a number of specimens of the organ that was missing in
the deceased. He stated his willingness to give £20 for each, and explained that his object
was to issue an actual specimen with each copy of a publication on which he was then
engaged. Although he was told that his wish was impossible to be complied with, he still
urged his request. He desired them preserved, not in spirits of wine, the usual medium,
but in glycerine, in order to preserve them in a flaccid condition, and he wished them sent
to America direct. It is known that this request was repeated to another institution of a
similar character. Now, is it not possible that the knowledge of this demand may have
incited some abandoned wretch to possess himself of a specimen. It seems beyond belief
that such inhuman wickedness could enter into the mind of any man, but unfortunately
our criminal annals prove that every crime is possible. I need hardly say that I at once
communicated my information to the Detective Department at Scotland Yard. Of course
I do not know what use has been made of it, but I believe that publicity may possibly
further elucidate this fact, and, therefore, I have not withheld from you my knowledge.
By means of the press some further explanation may be forthcoming from America if not
from here. I have endeavoured to suggest to you the object with which this offence was
committed, and the class of person who must have perpetrated it.

If your views accord with mine, you will be of the opinion that we are confronted with
a murder of no ordinary character, committed not from jealousy, revenge, or robbery, but
from motives less adequate than the many which still disgrace our civilisation, mar our
progress, and blot the pages of our Christianity. I cannot conclude my remarks without
thanking you for the attention you have given to the case, and the assistance you have
rendered me in our efforts to elucidate the truth of this horrible tragedy.

A verdict of wilful murder against a person or persons unknown was returned and the newspapers went wild with lurid descriptions and depictions of the 'Hanbury Street Horror.' Within hours of the murder, a broadsheet of doggerel verses entitled *Lines on the Terrible Tragedy* was being hawked on the streets by long song sellers, who cried out the verses to the hardly appropriate tune of 'My Village Home'.

Rumours became rife; one said the killer had scrawled 'Five, fifteen more and then I give myself up' on the fence above his handiwork on poor Annie. A leather apron discovered at the scene of the Hanbury Street murder – although later found not to be connected with the crime – led suspicion to fall upon anyone who used a knife or wore a leather apron for their trade, and, after the revelations of Dr Phillips, on the medical profession. Could the murderer be a man of medical learning – perhaps even a gentleman?

Following the repeated assertions in the press and on the streets that 'no Englishman could have perpetrated such a horrible crime', there were numerous cases of assault upon 'foreign types', especially members of the East End Jewish population. The *Daily News* expanded the story to claim the divisional police surgeon (George Bagster Phillips) and his assistant were 'out of their beds nearly all Saturday night on cases of assault.' The paper sensationally concluded, 'there may soon be murders from panic to add to murders from lust for blood… a touch will fire the whole district, in the mood which it is in now.'

Dissatisfied with police progress and concerned for the safety of the inhabitabts of the East End, a disparate body of interested parties, from tradesmen to labourers, gathered at The Crown public house on Mile End Road on 10 September 1888 to form the Whitechapel Vigilance Committee. At the meeting local vestryman George Lusk was appointed their chairman and Joseph Aarons, the licensee of The Crown, their treasurer.

On 10 September 1888 Detective Inspector Abberline, who was leading the hunt for the Whitechapel Murderer on the ground, drew a crowd at Commercial Street police station. He had arrived hotfoot from Gravesend with a suspect. William Piggott was apprehended for being seen drinking in a pub wearing a bloodstained shirt. He was known to Gravesend police for his strange behaviour, but he was not identified by police witnesses – and within two hours his speech had become so garbled a doctor was sent for to assess his sanity. Piggott was pronounced insane and was immediately removed to the asylum at Bow.

Following concerns expressed to the authorities by Dr Cowan and Dr Crabb about a certain Jacob Isenschmid, the police at Holloway succeeded in making an arrest and Detective Inspector Styles was sent to investigate this potential suspect. After Isenschmid was brought into custody, he was certified as a lunatic and was sent, under restraint, to Islington Workhouse (and later the Grove Hall Lunatic Asylum).

On 18 September 1888 PC John Johnson (number 866 of the City force), was on duty in the Minories at about 3 a.m. when he heard loud screams of 'Murder!' coming from a dark court. Running towards the cries, he was led to Butcher's Row and some railway arches near Whitechapel Road, where he found a man behaving in a threatening manner towards a prostitute named Elizabeth Burns. Asked what

BLIND-MAN'S BUFF.
(As played by the Police.)
"TURN ROUND THREE TIMES,
AND CATCH WHOM YOU MAY!"

As the investigation into the Ripper crimes failed to apprehend the murderer and the crimes continued, the police were widely criticised for inefficiency – as demonstrated by the mercilessly satirical cartoons of *Punch*, such as this jibe from 22 September 1888.

he was doing, the man replied 'nothing', but the distressed unfortunate begged, 'Oh, policeman, do take me out of this.' PC Johnson sent the man on his way and walked with the woman, who was too shaken to speak properly, to the end of his beat, when she blurted out, 'Dear me, he frightened me very much when he pulled that big knife out.' The constable set out in pursuit of the man but he could not be found. The man was later apprehended, at about 3 a.m., after an altercation at a coffee stall where he drew a knife and threatened Alexander Finlay (also known as Freinburg), who then threw a dish at the threatening man. PC John Gallagher 221H intervened and arrested the man, who was subsequently identified as German immigrant Charles Ludwig. Ludwig was held for a fortnight until his hearing at Thames Magistrates Court. Being in custody at the time of the murders of Stride and Eddowes, Ludwig had solid alibis for the latest Ripper killings. Magistrates considered he had been incarcerated long enough for his crimes and released him.

On 19 September Sir Charles Warren sent a report to the Home Office discussing the suspect Isenschmid (which Warren spells Isensmith) and a certain Oswald Puckeridge who had been released from an asylum on 4 August. Puckeridge had been educated as a surgeon and had been known to threaten to rip people up with a long knife. In the report Warren stated:

He is being looked for but cannot be found yet... A brothel keeper who will not give her address or name writes to say that a man living in her house was seen with blood on him on the morning of the murder... when the detectives came near him he bolted, got away and there is no clue to the writer of the letter.

Never one to miss a chance to publicise the plight of his flock, Samuel Barnett, canon of St Jude's and founder warden of Toynbee Hall, wrote an extended letter to *The Times* published on 19 September 1888. His arguments were clear: there should be a national effort to re-house the poor because such was degradation in which many in the East End lived, especially Spitalfields, that crime was inevitable. Part of his letter stated; 'Whitechapel horrors will not be in vain, if "at last" public conscience awakes to consider the life which these horrors reveal. The murders were, it may also be said, bound to come; generation could not follow generation in lawless intercourse.'

The Revd Barnett then made four practical suggestions to avoid the perpetuation of the situation:

1. Efficient police supervision.
2. Adequate lighting and cleaning.
3. The removal of slaughterhouses (sights such as blood on the streets from the butcher's and slaughterhouses brutalise ignorant natures).
4. The control of tenement houses by responsible landlords.

There was no groundswell from government or the people of Britain to improve the lot of the poverty stricken in the East End, but Canon Barnett never lost hope and worked tirelessly with local council, charities, benevolent individuals and organisations aimed at improving the life of those living in the poorest quarters of the East End.

September 27 1888 was literally a red-letter day for the Whitechapel murder case, for this was the date postmarked on the famous letter received at the offices of the Central News Agency, 5 New Bridge Street, Ludgate Circus. Posted in EC1 (East London), it read:

Dear Boss,

I keep on hearing the police have caught me but they wont [*sic*] fix me just yet. I have laughed when they look so clever and talk about being on the right track. That joke about Leather Apron gave me real fits. I am down on whores and I shant [*sic*] quit ripping them till I do get buckled. Grand work the last job was, I gave the lady no time to squeal. How can they catch me now. I love my work and want to start again. You will soon hear of me with my funny little games. I saved some of the proper red stuff in a ginger beer bottle over the last job to write with but it went thick like glue and I cant [*sic*] use it. Red ink is fit enough I hope ha ha. The next job I do I shall clip the ladys [*sic*] ears off and send to the police officers just for jolly wouldn't you. Keep this letter back till I do a bit more work then give it out straight. My knife's so nice and sharp I want to get to work right away if I get a chance. Good luck.

Yours truly
Jack the Ripper

Don't mind me giving the trade name. Wasn't good enough to post this before I got all the red ink off my hands curse it. No luck yet. They say I'm a doctor now ha ha.

This lurid missive would become known as the 'Dear Boss' letter. It was more likely to have been penned by an unscrupulous journalist hoping to add yet another twist to the tale than the actual murderer. The theme took off and soon hundreds of letters were being sent to London and provincial police forces and civic officials purporting to come from the Whitechapel Murderer. This letter will, however, remain unique and would go down in infamy as the first appearance of the name 'Jack the Ripper'.

On 29 September *Punch* magazine captured the mood with an eerie cartoon showing a spectre stalking the mean streets of the metropolis, the word 'CRIME' emblazoned on the forehead of the shroud it was wearing. The accompanying script contained this poem:

Foulness filters here from honest homes
And thievish dens, town-rookery, rural village.
Vice to be nursed to violence hither comes,
Nurture unnatural, abhorrent tillage!
What sin soever amidst luxury springs,
Here amidst poverty finds full fruition.
There is no name for the unsexed foul things
Plunged to their last perdition
In this dark Malebolge, ours–which yet
We build, and populate, and then–forget!

Dank roofs, dark entries, closely-clustered walls,
Murder-inviting nooks, death-reeking gutters,
A boding voice from your foul chaos calls,
When will men heed the warning that it utters?
There floats a phantom on the slum's foul air,
Shaping, to eyes which have the gift of seeing,
Into the Spectre of that loathly lair.
Face it–for vain is fleeing!
Red-handed, ruthless, furtive, unerect,
'Tis murderous Crime–the Nemesis of Neglect!

The following day, 30 September 1888, at 12.45 a.m., Israel Schwartz followed a man who appeared to be drunk into Berner Street from Commercial Road. As the man walked along the road he was seen to stop and speak with a woman later identified as 45-year-old Elizabeth Stride. Born Elisabeth Gustafsdotter, near Gothenburg, Sweden, she was commonly known on the streets of the East End as 'Long Liz'. Schwartz saw the man throw her to the ground and attempt to pull her onto the path outside Dutfield's Yard beside the International Workmen's Club. She screamed three times, but not very loudly. Schwartz wanted no part in this strife and crossed to the other side of the road, where he saw a man lighting his pipe. The man who threw the woman down could see Schwartz was staring and he shouted the typical abusive

The infamous 'Nemesis of Neglect' cartoon published in *Punch* magazine on the day before the 'Double Event.'

name for East End Jews at the time, 'Lipski', after the murderer of Miriam Angel in 1887 (see Chapter 3).

The man began to follow Schwartz, so Schwartz ran off. Later that night, at 1 a.m., Louis Diemshutz was returning to Dutfield's Yard with his costermonger's barrow, but as his pony entered it shied and would not walk on. Diemshutz went to investigate and saw what he thought was a pile of old clothes laying in the yard. He struck a match, and although it was almost instantly blown out by the wind he had seen enough. It was the body of a woman, later identified as Elizabeth Stride. Her throat had been slashed across, but she had not been mutilated – many drew the conclusion that Jack had been disturbed. However, if Jack had not had his hideous appetite for mutilation sated, he soon found his second victim.

Earlier that same evening Kate Eddowes (43) had been arrested for being drunk and disorderly outside 29 Aldgate High Street. Kate was described by her contemporaries as an educated woman but one with a fierce temper. Her marriage to George Eddowes had failed on account of her drinking. For a time she lived with another man, Thomas Conway, as man and wife. They had three children, but this relationship had also failed about six or seven years previously, also due to Eddowes' drinking. Conway was known to become violent towards her when he had had a drink. Eddowes left

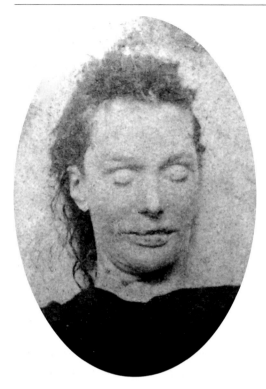

Mortuary photograph of
Elizabeth 'Long Liz' Stride.
(*Stewart P. Evans*)

and exhausted the good will of her family with her constant appeals for money and
her excessive drinking. When her relatives moved and kept their addresses from her,
Eddowes soon fell on hard times and took to living in dosshouses, drinking and
turning to prostitution as an occasional means of earning money. She had recently
returned from a trip to the hop-picking fields of Kent with her man friend, John
Kelly, described at the time as a 'strong looking labourer.' Things had not gone well
and they decided to return to London. Kelly later recalled, 'We did not have money
enough to keep us going till we got to town, but we did get there… Luck was dead
against us… we were both done up for cash.'

They reached London and spent a night together in a casual ward and the following
day John managed to earn 6*d*; at the inquest he recalled saying, '"Here, Kate, you
take 4*d* and go to the lodging-house and I will go to Mile End," but she said, "No,
you go and have a bed and I will go to the casual ward," and she went. I saw her
again on Saturday (29 September) morning early.'

Kelly decided to pawn a pair of his boots: Eddowes took them to the pawnbroker's
shop and received 2*s* 6*d*, pledging them under the name Jane Kelly. Eddowes and
Kelly bought some tea and sugar and ate a breakfast in the lodging-house kitchen.

By afternoon they were again without money. Kelly last saw Eddowes alive at
about two o'clock in the afternoon, in Houndsditch. They parted on good terms, with
Eddowes saying she was going over to Bermondsey to try and find her daughter Annie
(from her previous relationship with Thomas Conway) to get some money from her.

Eddowes had promised Kelly that she would be back by 4 p.m. and no later. She did not return.

The next record of Eddowes is her arrest by City Constable Lewis Robinson (931), at 8.30 p.m. on the night of Saturday 29 September on Aldgate High Street. He had seen a crowd gather outside No. 29 where he discovered Eddowes drunk and lying on the footway. He then picked her up and propped her against the shutters, but she fell down sideways. With the aid of a fellow-constable, Robinson took her to Bishopsgate police station. When Robinson asked her name, she replied, 'Nothing.' Eddowes was then placed in a cell.

And therein lay her fate. If she had been arrested for drunk and disorderly behaviour in the Metropolitan Police area she would have been put in the cells until the following morning; the City Police discharged drunks when they had sobered up. City Constable George Henry Hutt, 968, the gaoler at Bishopsgate station, took over the cells at 9.45 p.m. and, as per regulations, visited Eddowes in her cell several times, roughly every half hour: at first she remained asleep, but at 11.45 p.m. she was awake, and singing a song to herself. At 12.30 a.m. she asked when she would be able to leave. Hutt replied, 'Shortly.' To which she said, 'I am capable of taking care of myself now.' At 12.55 a.m. on Sunday morning, the inspector being out visiting, Hutt was directed by Sergeant Byfield to see if any of the prisoners were fit to be discharged. Finding Eddowes sober, and after she had given her name and address as Mary Ann Kelly, No. 6, Fashion-street, Spitalfields, she was allowed to leave.

At about 12.58 a.m., when Hutt was taking her out of the cell, Eddowes asked him what time it was. Hutt answered, 'Too late for you to get any more drink.' To which she replied, 'Well, what time is it?' He replied, 'Just on one.' Thereupon she said, 'I shall get a — fine hiding when I get home, then.' Hutt reprimanded her: 'Serve you right; you have no right to get drunk.' Hutt then pushed open the swing-door leading to the passage, and said, 'This way, missus.' And Eddowes walked along the passage to the outer door. At the inquest Hutt recalled, 'I said to her, "Please, pull it to." She replied, "All right. Good night, old cock." She pulled the door to within a foot of being closed, and I saw her turn to the left [towards Houndsditch].'

Just 400 yards from Bishopsgate police station is Mitre Square and there at 1.45 a.m. that same night PC Edward Watkins 881 discovered the hideously mutilated body of Kate Eddowes.

Major Henry Smith, the Acting Police Commissioner for the City of London force, recalled what happened next in his memoirs, *From Constable to Commissioner*, published in 1910:

> The night of Saturday, 29 September, found me tossing about in my bed at Cloak Lane Station, close to the river and adjoining Southwark Bridge. There was a railway goods depot in front, and a furrier's premises behind my rooms; the lane was causewayed, heavy vans were going constantly in and out, and the sickening smell from the furrier's skins was always present. You could not open the windows, and to sleep was an impossibility. Suddenly the bell at my head rang violently.

The Illustrated Police News graphically reports the 'Double Event' of 30 September 1888.

'What is it?' I asked, putting my ear to the tube.

'Another murder, sir, this time in the City.' Jumping up, I was dressed and in the street in a couple of minutes. A hansom – to me a detestable vehicle – was at the door, and into it I jumped, as time was of the utmost consequence. This invention of the devil claims to be safe. It is neither safe nor pleasant. In winter you are frozen; in summer you are broiled. When the glass is let down your hat is generally smashed, your fingers caught between the doors, or half your front teeth loosened. Licensed to carry two, it did not take me long to discover that a 15-stone Superintendent inside with me, and three detectives hanging on behind, added neither to its comfort nor to its safety.

Although we rolled like a 'seventy-four' in a gale, we got to our destination – Mitre Square – without an upset, where I found a small group of my men standing round the mutilated remains of a woman … The approaches to Mitre Square are three-by Mitre Street, Duke Street, and St James's Place. In the south-western corner, to which there is no approach, lay the woman.

Dr Frederick Gordon Brown, City Police surgeon, arrived at Mitre Square around 2 a.m. His report contained a description of the most hideous and extensive mutilations inflicted by the Ripper to date:

The body was on its back, the head turned to left shoulder. The arms by the side of the body as if they had fallen there. Both palms upwards, the fingers slightly bent. The left leg extended in a line with the body. The abdomen was exposed. Right leg bent at the thigh and knee. The throat cut across.

The intestines were drawn out to a large extent and placed over the right shoulder – they were smeared over with some feculent matter. A piece of about 2ft was quite detached from the body and placed between the body and the left arm, apparently by design. The lobe and auricle of the right ear were cut obliquely through.

Body was quite warm. No death stiffening had taken place. She must have been dead most likely within the half hour. We looked for superficial bruises and saw none. No blood on the skin of the abdomen or secretion of any kind on the thighs. No spurting of blood on the bricks or pavement around. No marks of blood below the middle of the body. Several buttons were found in the clotted blood after the body was removed. There was no blood on the front of the clothes. There were no traces of recent connexion.

When the body arrived at Golden Lane, some of the blood was dispersed through the removal of the body to the mortuary. The clothes were taken off carefully from the body. A piece of deceased's ear dropped from the clothing.

The face was very much mutilated. There was a cut about a quarter of an inch through the lower left eyelid, dividing the structures completely through. The upper eyelid on that side, there was a scratch through the skin on the left upper eyelid, near to the angle of the nose. The right eyelid was cut through to about half an inch.

There was a deep cut over the bridge of the nose, extending from the left border of the nasal bone down near the angle of the jaw on the right side of the cheek. This cut went into the bone and divided all the structures of the cheek except the mucous membrane of the mouth.

The tip of the nose was quite detached by an oblique cut from the bottom of the nasal bone to where the wings of the nose join on to the face. A cut from this divided the upper lip and extended through the substance of the gum over the right upper lateral incisor tooth.

About half an inch from the top of the nose was another oblique cut. There was a cut on the right angle of the mouth as if the cut of a point of a knife. The cut extended an inch and a half, parallel with the lower lip.

There was on each side of cheek a cut which peeled up the skin, forming a triangular flap about an inch and a half. On the left cheek there were two abrasions of the epithelium under the left ear.

The throat was cut across to the extent of about 6in or 7in. A superficial cut commenced about an inch and a half below the lobe below, and about 2½in behind the left ear, and extended across the throat to about 3in below the lobe of the right ear.

The big muscle across the throat was divided through on the left side. The large vessels on the left side of the neck were severed. The larynx was severed below the vocal chord. All the deep structures were severed to the bone, the knife marking intervertebral cartilages. The sheath of the vessels on the right side was just opened.

The carotid artery had a fine hole opening, the internal jugular vein was opened about an inch and a half – not divided. The blood vessels contained clot. All these injuries were performed by a sharp instrument like a knife, and pointed.

The cause of death was haemorrhage from the left common carotid artery. The death was immediate and the mutilations were inflicted after death.

The intestines had been detached to a large extent from the mesentery. About 2ft of the colon was cut away. Right kidney was pale, bloodless with slight congestion of the base of the pyramids.

There was a cut from the upper part of the slit on the under surface of the liver to the left side, and another cut at right angles to this, which were about an inch and a half deep and 2½in long. Liver itself was healthy.

The peritoneal lining was cut through on the left side and the left kidney carefully taken out and removed. The left renal artery was cut through. I would say that someone who knew the position of the kidney must have done it.

The lining membrane over the uterus was cut through. The womb was cut through horizontally, leaving a stump of three quarters of an inch. The rest of the womb had been taken away with some of the ligaments. I believe the wound in the throat was first inflicted. I believe she must have been lying on the ground.

The wounds on the face and abdomen prove that they were inflicted by a sharp, pointed knife, and that in the abdomen by one 6in or longer.

I believe the perpetrator of the act must have had considerable knowledge of the position of the organs in the abdominal cavity and the way of removing them. It required a great deal of medical knowledge to have removed the kidney and to know where it was placed. The parts removed would be of no use for any professional purpose.

I think the perpetrator of this act had sufficient time, or he would not have nicked the lower eyelids. It would take at least five minutes.

I cannot assign any reason for the parts being taken away. I feel sure that there was no struggle, and believe it was the act of one person.

The throat had been so instantly severed that no noise could have been emitted. I should not expect much blood to have been found on the person who had inflicted these wounds.

This night of macabre events was concluded with a discovery made by PC Alfred Long of A Division (on attachment to H Division) in the doorway of 108–19 Wentworth Model Dwellings, Goulston Street. It was a piece of material torn from Kate's apron, smeared with blood and faeces, upon which the murderer had wiped his knife and hands. Dr Brown commented:

My attention was called to the apron, particularly the corner of the apron with a string attached. The blood spots were of recent origin. I have seen the portion of an apron produced by Dr Phillips and stated to have been found in Goulston Street. It is impossible to say that it is human blood on the apron. I fitted the piece of apron, which had a new piece of material on it (which had evidently been sewn on to the piece I have), the seams of the borders of the two actually corresponding.

Above the apron fragment, written 'in a good schoolboy hand', was the statement: 'The Juwes are the men that will not be blamed for nothing.' Two schools of thought enshroud this message: one suggests it was only a coincidence, that the rag was simply cast away by the murderer and just happened to land under the message; the other suggests it was a message left by the killer himself.

Sir Charles Warren, the Commissioner of the Metropolitan Police, attended the scene in person; no doubt fearing riots and reprisals against the Jewish population in the East End if such an inflammatory statement became popular knowledge, rather than wait until there was enough light to photograph the message he controversially overruled the other officers on the scene and only had the message copied down, personally giving a direct order to 'obliterate the writing at once.' Some accounts even claim Warren erased the message himself.

It was to be a controversial decision that would ultimately contribute to his later resignation. Warren recorded his reasons in a confidential letter to the Under Secretary of State, the Home Office, on 6 November 1888:

Sir,

In reply to your letter of the 5th instant, I enclose a report of the circumstances of the Mitre Square Murder so far as they have come under the notice of the Metropolitan Police, and I now give an account regarding the erasing of the writing on the wall in Goulston Street, which I have already partially explained to Mr Matthews verbally.

On 30 September, on hearing of the Berner Street murder, after visiting Commercial Street Station I arrived at Leman Street Station shortly before 5 a.m. and ascertained from the Superintendent Arnold all that was known there relative to the two murders.

The most pressing question at that moment was some writing on the wall in Goulston Street evidently written with the intention of inflaming the public mind against the Jews, and which Mr Arnold with a view to prevent serious disorder proposed to obliterate, and had sent down an Inspector with a sponge for that purpose, telling him to await his arrival.

I considered it desirable that I should decide the matter myself, as it was one involving so great a responsibility whether any action was taken or not.

I accordingly went down to Goulston Street at once before going to the scene of the murder: it was just getting light, the public would be in the streets in a few minutes, in a neighbourhood very much crowded on Sunday mornings by Jewish vendors and Christian purchasers from all parts of London.

There were several Police around the spot when I arrived, both Metropolitan and City.

The writing was on the jamb of the open archway or doorway visible *in the street* and could not be covered up without danger of the covering being torn off at once.

The Petticoat Lane market on Goulston Street in the late nineteenth century

A discussion took place whether the writing could be *left covered up* or otherwise or whether any portion of it could be left for an hour until it could be photographed; but after taking into consideration the excited state of the population in London generally at the time, the strong feeling which had been excited against the Jews, and the fact that in a short time there would be a large concourse of the people in the streets, and having before me the Report that if it was left there the house was likely to be wrecked (in which from my own observation I entirely concurred) I considered it desirable to obliterate the writing at once, having taken a copy of which I enclose a duplicate.

After having been to the scene of the murder, I went on to the City Police Office and informed the Chief Superintendent of the reason why the writing had been obliterated.

I may mention that so great was the feeling with regard to the Jews that on the 13th ulto. the Acting Chief Rabbi wrote to me on the subject of the spelling of the word 'Jewes' on account of a newspaper asserting that this was Jewish spelling in the Yiddish dialect. He added 'in the present state of excitement it is dangerous to the safety of the poor Jews in the East to allow such an assertion to remain uncontradicted. My community keenly appreciates your humane and vigilant action during this critical time.'

It may be realised therefore if the safety of the Jews in Whitechapel could be considered to be jeopardised thirteen days after the murder by the question of the spelling of the word Jews, what might have happened to the Jews in that quarter had that writing been left intact.

I do not hesitate myself to say that if that writing had been left there would have been an onslaught upon the Jews, property would have been wrecked, and lives would probably have been lost; and I was much gratified with the promptitude with which Superintendent Arnold was prepared to act in the matter if I had not been there.

I have no doubt myself whatever that one of the principal objects of the Reward offered by Mr Montagu was to shew to the world that the Jews were desirous of having the Hanbury Street Murder cleared up, and thus to divert from them the very strong feeling which was then growing up.

I am, Sir,

Your most obedient Servant,

Charles Warren

Shortly after the Ripper's 'Double Event' on 30 September, a lurid pamphlet entitled *The Curse of Mitre Square* began to be circulated on the streets of the East End. It stated the Square had been damned since the murder of another woman on exactly the same spot by a mad monk (known as Brother Martin) in 1530. It is true to say that Mitre Square was indeed the site of the Priory of the Holy Trinity, founded in 1108 and dissolved in 1540, but the broadsheet goes on to state that a woman who was praying before the high altar had been attacked by the insane monk: his knife 'descended with lightening rapidity, and pools of blood deluged the altar steps. With a demon's fury the monk then threw down the corpse and trod it out of recognition.'

Brother Martin then plunged the knife into his own heart. As the spot remained unhallowed, the Ripper simply fulfilled the ancient curse – so the author of the broadsheet argued. The police made door-to-door enquiries and posters were pasted up:

Police Notice:

To the Occupier.

On the mornings of Friday 31 August, Saturday 8, and Sunday 30 September 1888, Women were murdered in or near Whitechapel, supposed by some one residing in the immediate neighbourhood. Should you know of any person to whom suspicion is attached, you are earnestly requested to communicate at once with the nearest Police Station.

Metropolitan Police Office

30th September 1888

On 1 October 1888 a postcard smeared with blood and written in red ink was received by the Central News Agency. Its contents would immortalise the previous night's atrocities as 'The Double Event':

I was not codding dear old Boss when I gave you the tip. You'll hear about saucy Jacky's work tomorrow. Double event this time. Number one squealed a bit. Couldn't finish straight off. Had not time to get ears for police. Thanks for keeping back the last letter till I got to work again – Jack the Ripper.

On 2 October 1888 private investigators Grand and Batchelor (employed by the Whitechapel Vigilance Committee) found a bloodstained grape stalk in a drain near where the body of Elizabeth Stride was found. This information was not widely broadcast but when combined with the account of Matthew Packer (who ran a small greengrocers through a street window at 44 Berner Street) that he had served a man accompanied by Stride with half a pound of black grapes, the sale of the fruit entered into East End folklore. The grapes have taken on yet greater significance in recent years as imaginative theorists suggest the Ripper laced the grapes with laudanum to stupefy his victims prior to his attack. On this same day Robert James Lees, a medium, offered his powers as a psychic to assist the police. Lees indignantly recorded in his diary that he was sent away and 'called a fool and a lunatic.'

With little or no concept of forensic clues to assist with the detection of the murderer, and mounting pressure coming from all quarters for progress in tracking Jack the Ripper, new ideas and any new method which may have some merit were considered. Sir Charles Warren personally oversaw the trials of bloodhounds on Regents Park on 9 and 10 October. Two hounds, Barnaby and Burgho, were brought down to London from Scarborough by well-known breeder, Mr Brough. Sir Charles even acted as quarry in one of the trials and expressed himself satisfied with the result. The incident did however acquire a certain mythology when both hounds and Sir Charles got lost in the London smog.

As time passed, more and more suggestions of how the police could catch the Ripper or protect the women of London from the fiend were related in the letters columns of the press. Typical of the tenor and logic employed in the correspondence is the following from the *Pall Mall Gazette*:

> There are numbers of well trained pugilists in Shoreditch and Whitechapel who are, many of them, young, and in the custom in their profession, clean shaved... Twenty game men of this class in women's clothing loitering about Whitechapel would have more chance than any number of heavy-footed policemen.

That said, the police did start experiments with 'decoys' being used in attempts to draw out and capture Jack the Ripper. They were small in number but two clearly recorded decoys were Detective Sergeant Robinson (who took to the streets in 'veil, skirt and petticoats') and Detective Sergeant Mather, who remained in his plain clothes. Observing a man behaving in a strange manner with a woman in a doorway near Phoenix Place, St Pancras, the detectives were accused of being voyeurs by a passing cab washer named William Jarvis. Challenged with, 'Wot yer muckin' about ere for', the policemen identified themselves. 'Oh, a rozzer, eh?' Jarvis replied sceptically, and belted Robinson in the eye. Another decoy was a volunteer named Amelia Brown of Peckham who, although kept under close observation by policemen, was only issued with a police whistle for her personal protection.

From the moment the first Jack the Ripper letter arrived at the Central News Agency, a torrent of letters claiming to know, have knowledge of, or even purporting to be from Jack the Ripper were sent. Some were illustrated with lurid drawings and lots of red ink. Then, on 16 October 1888, George Lusk, Chairman of the Whitechapel Vigilance Committee, received a small parcel in the form of a cardboard box wrapped in brown paper. To Lusk's horror, upon opening the parcel he found the box contained a bloodstained letter and half a human kidney.

From Hell

Mr Lusk
Sor
I send you half the
Kidne I took from one woman
Preserved it for you, tother piece I
fried and ate it was very nise. I
may send you the bloody knife that
took it out if you only wate a whil
longer.

Signed: Catch me when you can
Mishter Lusk

The kidney was examined by Dr Openshaw at the London Hospital, who confirmed it was a longitudinally divided human kidney. Major Smith of the City Police added in his memoirs that 2in of the renal artery (averaging about 3in long) remained in Eddowes body where her kidney had been removed – one inch of artery was all that was attached to the organ sent to Lusk.

During the month of October the Victorian philanthropist Dr Thomas John Barnardo was to become involved in the story of Jack the Ripper. Writing an impassioned letter about the suffering of the children in common lodging houses to *The Times*, published on 9 October, he revealed:

Only four days before the recent murders I visited No. 32 Flower and Dean Street, the house in which the unhappy woman Stride occasionally lodged... In the kitchen of No. 32 there were many persons, some of them being girls and women of the same unhappy class that to which poor Elizabeth Stride belonged. The company soon recognised me, and the conversation turned upon the previous murders. The female inmates of the kitchen seemed thoroughly frightened at the dangers to which they were presumably exposed... One poor creature, who had evidently been drinking, exclaimed somewhat bitterly to the following effect: 'We're all up to no good, and no one cares what becomes of us. Perhaps some of us will be killed next!' I have since visited the mortuary in which were lying the remains of the poor woman Stride, and I at once recognised her as one of those who stood around me in the kitchen of the common lodging-house on the occasion of my visit last Wednesday week.

Also in October 1888, reports circulate of the curious circumstances surrounding the death of Mrs Mary Burridge, a floor-cloth dealer on the Blackfriars Road. It was stated by some she had been so overcome by reading a particularly lurid account of the Whitechapel Murders in the *Star* that she fell dead, '…a copy of the late final in her hand.' Tom Cullen, in *Jack the Ripper*, suggested this passage may have caught her eye: 'A nameless reprobate – half beast, half man – is at large… Hideous malice, deadly cunning, insatiable thirst for blood – all these are the marks of the mad homicide. The ghoul-like creature, stalking down his victim like a Pawnee Indian, is simply drunk with blood, and he will have more.'

American actor Richard Mansfield trod the boards of Henry Irving's Lyceum Theatre in his acclaimed stage adaptation of Robert Louis Stevenson's *Dr Jekyll and Mr Hyde*. Since the book was first published in 1886, Victorian sensibilities were outraged by the premise that every human being (even the respectable ones) has a demon imprisoned within them that the right concoctions of chemicals could release on society to gorge themselves on an orgy of debauchery and malevolence. Mansfield's transformation from the upright Dr Jekyll to hideous Mr Hyde 'in all his blood curdling repulsiveness' was remarked upon for the convincing and complete transformation of man to half human beast, a transformation made more shocking and horrible because it was done in full view of the audience without 'screens, gauzes or traps.'

Due to accusations that the play was responsible in some way for the Jack the Ripper murders (on the grounds of his performance, some even suspected Mansfield himself of being the Ripper), the run of the play was cut short and terminated in its tenth week.

So the investigation went on, but by November 1888 there was still no convincing suspect in sight, the streets of East London were gripped by terror and the nation was on tenterhooks, wondering not if, but when Jack the Ripper would strike again.

Further ingenious suggestions for the apprehension of Jack the Ripper (and appliances to be worn about the neck to prevent his deadly attack) were proffered. Mr W.H. Spencer summed up this theme in a letter printed in *The Star*:

… a few young men of somewhat feminine appearance should be got up in disguises as females. They should wear around their necks steel collars made after the style of a ladies' collaret, coming well down the breast and likewise well down the back. My reason for this is… that the assassin first severs his victim's windpipe, thereby preventing her raising an alarm.

The following letter was published in *The Daily Telegraph*:

Sir, Can nothing be done to prevent a set of hoarse ruffians coming nightly about our suburban squares and streets yelling at the tops of their voices, and nearly frightening the life out of sensitive women and children of this neighbourhood? Last evening, for instance, their cry was 'Special' – 'Murder' – 'Paper' – 'Jack' – 'The' – 'Ripper' –

Richard Mansfield in the guise of Dr Jeckyll's evil alter-ego Mr Hyde – a performance so convincing it was suggested his portrayal might be influencing the crimes of Jack the Ripper.

'Caught' – 'Paper' – 'Whitechapel' – 'Paper' – 'Got him at last' – 'Paper'... These awful words were bawled out about nine o' clock in a quiet part of Kensington; a lady who was supping with us was so greatly distressed by these hideous bellowings that she was absolutely too unnerved to return home save in a cab because she would have to walk 100 yards or so down a street at the end of her journey by omnibus. Now, I venture to ask sir, is it not monstrous that the police do not protect us from such flagrant and ghastly nuisances?

Then, just as the height of fear began to wane a little, came another murder. Mary Jane (or Marie Jeanette) Kelly was remembered as a striking figure in the East End. Known on the streets as 'Black Mary', she was younger than most of the prostitutes; she was twenty-five, blue-eyed, tall with a fine head of blonde hair almost reaching to her waist. She had come to London in 1884 and after a short period working as a domestic servant she became a high-class prostitute in a West End brothel. This life saw her turn to drink, and she soon found herself out of the brothel and down in the East End working as a common prostitute and living and working out of a dingy room, about 12ft square, at 13 Miller's Court. This property was colloquially known as one of 'McCarthy's Rents' – named after John McCarthy, who owned a chandler's shop at 27 Dorset Street and rented out a number of properties around the locale. Miller's Court itself was accessed through a narrow opening about 3ft wide; it was the first archway on the right off Dorset Street when approaching from Commercial Street.

In *Autumn of Terror* (1965), Tom Cullen recorded some of the memories of those who could recall Mary Kelly. Apparently her pitch was well known (in front of the Ten Bells on Commercial Street) – and woe betide any other unfortunate who trod on it, for she had brawled, 'pulling hair out by fistfuls', on a number of occasions.

Mary had been living from rent to rent in a few lodging houses with her man friend, Joe Barnett, since 1887. While at Miller's Court, Joe lost his job as a fish porter and Mary returned to the streets. She brought girls back to the room out of the cold but, as Joe told a newspaper, he could not tolerate any more after 'Marie allowed a prostitute named Julia to sleep in the same room. I objected, and as Mrs Harvey afterwards came and stayed there, I left and took lodgings elsewhere.' At the inquest Barnett stated he and Kelly separated on 30 October 1888. However, they remained in friendly contact, and Barnett last saw Mary at Miller's Court when he visited her there on the night of Thursday 8 November 1888. He stayed there for a quarter of an hour, leaving at about 8 p.m.

At about 11.45 p.m. on the same night, Mary was seen with another man, probably a client, in Miller's Court by fellow resident and prostitute, Mary Ann Cox. Kelly and the man were standing outside Kelly's room by Mrs Cox, who bade them 'Goodnight' as she passed. Somewhat incoherently, Kelly replied, 'Goodnight, I am going to sing.' A few minutes later Mrs Cox heard Kelly singing 'A Violet from Mother's Grave'. Cox went out again at midnight and heard Kelly singing the same song:

Well I remember my dear old mother's smile,
As she used to greet me when I returned from toil,
Always knitting in the old arm chair,
Father used to sit and read for all us children there,
But now all is silent around the good old home;
They all have left me in sorrow here to roam,
But while life does remain, in memoriam I'll retain
This small violet I pluck'd from mother's grave.

Chorus of the popular American song 'A Violet from Mother's Grave'.
Words and music by Will Fox, published by J.W. Pepper, Philadelphia, 1881.

The last witness to see Mary Kelly alive was an old acquaintance of hers named George Hutchinson. In a statement he gave to the police after the inquest, Hutchinson recounted his last sighting of Mary. At about 2 a.m. Hutchinson was walking on Commercial Street and passed a man at the corner of Thrawl Street but paid no attention to him. At Flower and Dean Street he met Kelly, who asked him to lend her sixpence. Hutchinson replied he could not, having spent all his money 'going down to Romford.' Mary replied, 'Good morning, I must go and find some money.' And she left in the direction of Thrawl Street. Hutchinson continued:

Mary Kelly's dingy rent at 13
Miller's Court – scene of the
most horrific murder committed
by Jack the Ripper.

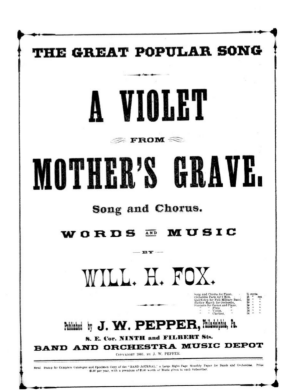

Cover of an original song sheet
for 'A Violet from Mother's
Grave' – the last song to be
heard sung by Mary Kelly.

A man coming in the opposite direction tapped her on the shoulder and said something to her, they both burst out laughing. I heard her say, 'All right?' to which the man replied, 'You will be alright for what I have told you.' The man then placed his right hand around her shoulders. He also had a kind of small parcel in his left hand with a kind of strap around it. I stood against the lamp of the Queens Head public house and watched him. They both then came past me the man hid down his head with his hat over his eyes. I stooped down and looked him in the face. He looked at me stern. They both went into Dorset Street. I followed them. They both stood at the corner of Miller's Court for about three minutes. He said something to her, she said, 'Alright my dear, come along, you will be comfortable.' He then placed his arm on her shoulder and gave her a kiss, then she said, 'I've lost me handkerchief.' He then pulled his handkerchief, a red one, out and gave it to her. They both then went up the court together. I then went to the court to see if I could see them but could not. I stood there for about three quarters of an hour to see if they came out but they did not and so I went away.

Did George Hutchinson get a good look at Jack the Ripper? And even if he did, was the description he gave accurate? It must be commented that for the short period of time he saw the man, the description he gave is remarkably detailed. The accuracy of Hutchinson's statement will no doubt be debated for years to come; if it is to be believed, then it is probably the best description we have of Jack the Ripper. The description he gave was as follows:

Aged about 34 or 35, height 5ft 6in, complexion pale, dark eyes and eye lashes, slight moustache curled up each end and hair dark, very surly looking, dressed in a long dark coat, collar and cuffs trimmed with astracan, and a dark jacket under, light waistcoat, dark trousers, dark felt hat, turned down in the middle, button boots and gaiters with white buttons. Wore a very thick gold chain and had a white linen collar, black tie with horse shoe pin, respectable appearance, walked very sharp, Jewish appearance. I think I would be able to identify him again.

But what happened to Mary? At about 4 a.m. on Friday 9 November, Elizabeth Prater was awakened by her pet kitten walking on her neck. She heard a faint cry of 'Oh, murder!' but could not be sure where it came from – and as the cry of murder was common in the district, she paid no attention to it. Sarah Lewis, who was staying with friends in Miller's Court, also heard the cry.

Later that morning ex-soldier Thomas Bowyer (known on the street as Indian Harry) was sent round to 13 Miller's Court by McCarthy to chase up Mary Kelly; she was behind with her rent money to the tune of 29s and was facing eviction.

At the inquest into the death of Mary Kelly held at Shoreditch Town Hall, before Dr Macdonald, MP, the coroner for the North-Eastern District of Middlesex, Bowyer deposed:

One of the most evocative images from
The Illustrated Police News – Mary Kelly
opens the door to admit death.

At a quarter to eleven a.m., on Friday morning (9 November), I was ordered by
McCarthy to go to Mary Jane's room, No. 13. I did not know the deceased by the name
of Kelly. I went for rent, which was in arrears. Knocking at the door, I got no answer, and
I knocked again and again. Receiving no reply, I passed round the corner by the gutter
spout where there is a broken window – it is the smallest window.

Charles Ledger, an inspector of police, G Division, produced a plan of the
premises. Bowyer pointed out the window, which was the one nearest the entrance.
Bowyer continued:

There was a curtain. I put my hand through the broken pane and lifted the curtain. I saw
two pieces of flesh lying on the table... in front of the bed, close to it. The second time
I looked I saw a body on this bed, and blood on the floor. I at once went very quietly to
Mr McCarthy. We then stood in the shop, and I told him what I had seen. We both went
to the police station, but first of all we went to the window, and McCarthy looked in to
satisfy himself. We told the inspector at the police station of what we had seen. Nobody
else knew of the matter. The inspector returned with us.

Inspector Frederick Abberline picked up the story with his testimony:

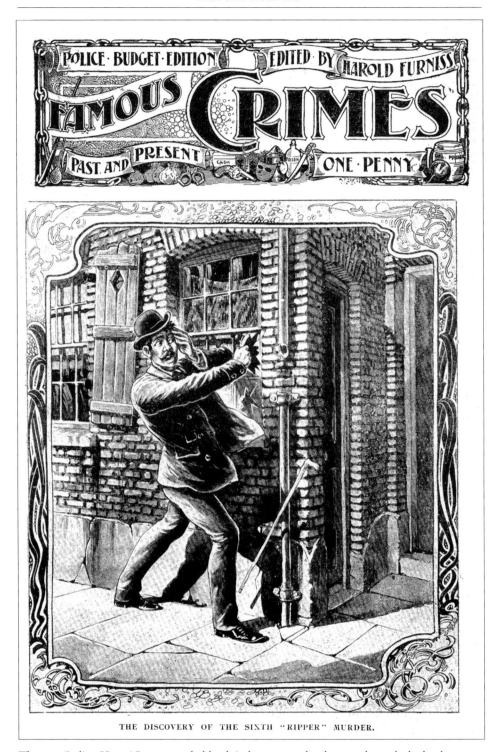

THE DISCOVERY OF THE SIXTH "RIPPER" MURDER.

Thomas 'Indian Harry' Bowyer reeled back in horror at what he saw through the broken window pane of No. 13 Miller's Court.

I arrived at Miller's Court about 11.30 on Friday morning … I had an intimation from Inspector Beck that the bloodhounds had been sent for, and the reply had been received that they were on the way. Dr Phillips was unwilling to force the door, as it would be very much better to test the dogs, if they were coming. We remained until about 1.30 p.m., when Superintendent Arnold arrived, and he informed me that the order in regard to the dogs had been countermanded, and he gave orders for the door to be forced…

The sight that met them was beyond human imagination – the walls were splashed up like an abattoir and on the blood-soaked mattress was a raw carcass, a mass of human evisceration that was once Mary Kelly. Those who saw this horror – Inspector Walter Beck, Inspector Frederick Abberline, George Bagster Phillips, the H Division surgeon, and even young PC Walter Dew (who would later become world famous as the man who arrested Dr Crippen) – would never forget what they saw at Miller's Court.

Dr Thomas Bond also attended the scene and recorded the state of the body of poor Mary Kelly:

The body was lying naked in the middle of the bed, the shoulders flat but the axis of the body inclined to the left side of the bed. The head was turned on the left cheek. The left arm was close to the body with the forearm flexed at a right angle and lying across the abdomen.

The right arm was slightly abducted from the body and rested on the mattress. The elbow was bent, the forearm supine with the fingers clenched. The legs were wide apart, the left thigh at right angles to the trunk and the right forming an obtuse angle with the pubes.

The whole of the surface of the abdomen and thighs was removed and the abdominal cavity emptied of its viscera. The breasts were cut off, the arms mutilated by several jagged wounds and the face hacked beyond recognition of the features. The tissues of the neck were severed all round down to the bone.

The viscera were found in various parts viz: the uterus and kidneys with one breast under the head, the other breast by the right foot, the liver between the feet, the intestines by the right side and the spleen by the left side of the body. The flaps removed from the abdomen and thighs were on a table.

The face was gashed in all directions, the nose, cheeks, eyebrows, and ears being partly removed. The lips were blanched and cut by several incisions running obliquely down to the chin. There were also numerous cuts extending irregularly across all the features.

The neck was cut through the skin and other tissues right down to the vertebrae, the fifth and sixth being deeply notched. The skin cuts in the front of the neck showed distinct ecchymosis. The air passage was cut at the lower part of the larynx through the cricoid cartilage.

Both breasts were more or less removed by circular incisions, the muscle down to the ribs being attached to the breasts. The intercostals between the fourth, fifth, and sixth ribs were cut through and the contents of the thorax visible through the openings.

The skin and tissues of the abdomen from the costal arch to the pubes were removed in three large flaps. The right thigh was denuded in front to the bone, the flap of skin, including the external organs of generation, and part of the right buttock. The left thigh was stripped of skin fascia, and muscles as far as the knee.

The left calf showed a long gash through skin and tissues to the deep muscles and reaching from the knee to 5in above the ankle. Both arms and forearms had extensive jagged wounds.

The pericardium was open below and the heart absent.

Inspector Abberline also commented during his inquest deposition:

I agree with the medical evidence as to the condition of the room. I subsequently took an inventory of the contents of the room. There were traces of a large fire having been kept up in the grate, so much so that it had melted the spout of a kettle off. We have since gone through the ashes in the fireplace; there were remnants of clothing, a portion of a brim of a hat, and a skirt, and it appeared as if a large quantity of women's clothing had been burnt.

The coroner enquired if Abberline could give any reason why the clothing had been burnt. Abberline replied, 'I can only imagine that it was to make a light for the man [the killer] to see what he was doing.'

Mary Jane Kelly is widely regarded by crime historians as the last of the canonical five victims of Jack the Ripper. Poignantly, the resignation (tendered on 8 November) of Sir Charles Warren, the man many held responsible for the failure of the police to capture Jack the Ripper, was accepted and announced on this day. But the investigation carried on and the following notice was issued:

MURDER-PARDON
Whereas on November 8 or 9, in Miller Court, Dorset Street, Spitalfields, Mary Jane Kelly was murdered by some person or persons unknown, the Secretary of State will advise the grant of her Majesty's pardon to any accomplice not being a person who contrived or actually committed the murder who shall give such information and evidence as shall lead to the discovery and conviction of the person or persons who committed the murder
(Signed) CHARLES WARREN, the Commissioner of Police of the Metropolis, Metropolitan Police Office, 4, Whitehall, November 10, 1888.

Even Queen Victoria sent a telegram from Balmoral to the Marquis of Salisbury, the Prime Minister, expressing her concern and suggesting actions to apprehend Jack the Ripper:

This new most ghastly murder shows the absolute necessity for some very decided action. All courts must be lit, & our detectives improved. They are not what they should be...

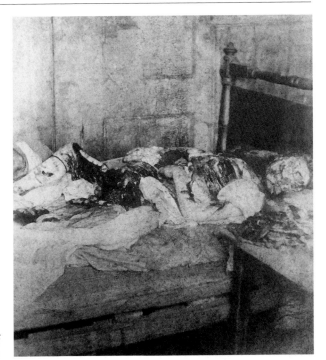

One of the first ever police crime scene photographs: the hideously mutilated remains of Mary Kelly. (*Stewart P. Evans*)

The Illustrated Police News recalls the recent murders and shows a depiction of the supposed 'Whitechapel Monster' based on the description given by George Hutchinson.

The killer known as Jack the Ripper was never brought to justice, but the case remained open, and a few suspects contemporary to the crimes were named by senior police officers in the years immediately after.

In 1891 a certain Thomas Henry Cutbush was taken into Lambeth Infirmary and detained as a lunatic. He escaped within hours and over the following four days until he was captured he stabbed Florrie Johnson in the buttocks and attempted to repeat the deed on Isabelle Anderson. Charged with malicious wounding, Cutbush spent the rest of his life in Broadmoor Criminal Lunatic Asylum, where he died in 1903. In February 1894 the *Sun* newspaper made the suggestion that Cutbush and Jack the Ripper were one and the same. This matter was thoroughly investigated and Cutbush was not considered a likely suspect at all. This investigation did however result in Sir Melville Macnaghten, Assistant Chief Constable CID, writing his confidential and now infamous report. Although not in post in 1888, he was appointed in 1889 when the crime, and what evidence there was available, was still fresh. He stated:

The Whitechapel murderer had 5 victims – & 5 victims only, – his murders were:
(1) 31st August, '88. Mary Ann Nichols – at Buck's Row – who was found with her throat cut – & with (slight) stomach mutilation.
(2) 8th Sept. '88 Annie Chapman – Hanbury St.; – throat cut – stomach & private parts badly mutilated & some of the entrails placed round the neck.
(3) 30th Sept. '88. Elizabeth Stride – Berner's Street – throat cut, but nothing in shape of mutilation attempted, & *on same date*
Catherine Eddowes – Mitre Square, throat cut & very bad mutilation, both of face and stomach.

Sir Melville Leslie Macnaghten. (*Stewart P. Evans*)

(4) 9th November. Mary Jane Kelly – Miller's Court, throat cut, and the whole of the
body mutilated in the most ghastly manner –

The last murder is the only one that took place in a *room*, and the murderer must have
been at least 2 hours engaged. A photo was taken of the woman, as she was found lying
on the bed, without seeing which it is impossible to imagine the awful mutilation.

With regard to the *double* murder which took place on 30th September, there is no
doubt but that the man was disturbed by some Jews who drove up to a Club, (close to
which the body of Elizabeth Stride was found) and that he then, *'mordum satiatus'*, went
in search of a further victim who he found at Mitre Square.

It will be noted that the fury of the mutilations *increased* in each case, and, seemingly,
the appetite only became sharpened by indulgence. It seems, then, highly improbable
that the murderer would have suddenly stopped in November '88, and been content
to recommence operations by merely prodding a girl's behind some two years and four
months afterwards. A much more rational theory is that the murderer's brain gave way
altogether after his awful glut in Miller's Court, and that he immediately committed
suicide, or, as a possible alternative, was found to be so hopelessly mad by his relations,
that he was by them confined in some asylum.

No one ever saw the Whitechapel murderer; many homicidal maniacs were suspected,
but no shadow of proof could be thrown on any one. I may mention the cases of three
men, any one of whom would have been more likely than Cutbush to have committed
this series of murders:

(1) A Mr M.J. Druitt, said to be a doctor & of good family – who disappeared at the time
of the Miller's Court murder, & whose body (which was said to have been upwards
of a month in the water) was found in the Thames on 31st December – or about seven
weeks after that murder. He was sexually insane and from private information I have
little doubt but that his own family believed him to have been the murderer.

(2) Kosminski – a Polish Jew – & resident in Whitechapel. This man became insane
owing to many years indulgence in solitary vices. He had a great hatred of women,
specially of the prostitute class, & had strong homicidal tendencies: he was removed
to a lunatic asylum about March 1889. There were many circumstances connected
with this man which made him a strong 'suspect'.

(3) Michael Ostrog, a Russian doctor, and a convict, who was subsequently detained
in a lunatic asylum as a homicidal maniac. This man's antecedents were of the
worst possible type, and his whereabouts at the time of the murders could never
be ascertained.

Macnaghten also went on to discuss other murdered women alleged to have been
victims of Jack the Ripper:

(1) The body of Martha Tabram, a prostitute was found on a common staircase in
George Yard buildings on 7th August 1888; the body had been repeatedly *pierced*,
probably with a *bayonet*. This woman had, with a fellow prostitute, been in company

Montague John Druitt.

Police Gazette wanted notice for Michael Ostrog. (*Stewart P. Evans*)

of 2 soldiers in the early part of the evening: these men were arrested, but the second prostitute failed, or refused, to identify, and the soldiers were eventually discharged.

(2) Alice McKenzie was found with her throat cut (or rather *stabbed*) in Castle Alley on 17th July 1889; no evidence was forthcoming and no arrests were made in connection with this case. The *stab* in the throat was of the same nature as in the case of the murder of

(3) Frances Coles in Swallow Gardens, on 13th February 1891 – for which Thomas Sadler, a fireman, was arrested, and, after several remands, discharged. It was ascertained at the time that Saddler had sailed for the Baltic on 19th July '89 and was in Whitechapel on the nights of 17th idem. He was a man of ungovernable temper and entirely addicted to drink, and the company of the lowest prostitutes.

Another suspect was advanced by Chief Inspector Frederick Abberline, the officer who led the Ripper investigation 'at ground level' in Whitechapel. He retired in 1892 and a few of his reminiscences were recorded to mark the occasion in *Cassell's Saturday Journal*. He sums up his views on the Ripper murders with '...we were lost almost in theories; there were so many of them.' But in 1903 Abberline recorded his own theory for the first time in *Pall Mall Gazette*. With George Chapman (AKA Severin Klosowski) 'The Borough Poisoner' under sentence of death when the reporter called on him, Abberline was planning to write to Metropolitan Police Commissioner Sir Melville Macnaghten '...to say how strongly I was impressed with the opinion that "Chapman" was also the author of the Whitechapel murders.' Drawing on a sheaf of papers and cuttings, Abberline passed his conclusions, which he had intended to send to Macnaghten directly, to the reporter. The letter covered a page and a half of foolscap paper and it outlined the coincidences, especially how the murders had continued in America (Chapman had emigrated to New Jersey in 1891), how they mirrored Chapman's movements and how struck he was with how Chapman could fit the descriptions they had of the Ripper at the time.

Sadly, most of Abberline's thoughts about Chapman as the Ripper do not withstand close scrutiny. Chapman was indeed a killer, but he was a poisoner and probably was not Jack the Ripper – but if it gave Abberline peace of mind in his declining years that his old comrade Detective Sergeant Godley had been the man to catch Jack the Ripper, who are we to judge?

Then there is the Littlechild letter. Discovered by crime historian Stewart P. Evans in 1993, it is a letter written on 23 September 1913 to the noted author, playwright and journalist George R. Sims from ex-Chief Inspector John Littlechild, the former head of Special Branch from 1883 to 1893. In the letter Littlechild discusses the infamous Jack the Ripper letter sent to the Central News Agency in 1888, which gave the murderer the most notorious *nom de plume* in history:

With regard to the term 'Jack the Ripper' it was generally believed at the Yard that Tom Bullen [*sic*] of the Central News was the originator, but it is probable Moore, who was his chief, was the inventor. It was a smart piece of journalistic work. No journalist of my

George Chapman.

time got such privileges from Scotland Yard as Bullen. Mr James Munro when Assistant Commissioner, and afterwards Commissioner, relied on his integrity. Poor Bullen occasionally took too much to drink, and I fail to see how he could help it knocking about so many hours and seeking favours from so many people to procure copy.

But, more significantly, Littlechild named another suspect:

Knowing the great interest you take in all matters criminal, and abnormal, I am just going to inflict one more letter on you on the 'Ripper' subject. Letters as a rule are only a nuisance when they call for a reply but this does not need one. I will try and be brief.

I never heard of a Dr D. in connection with the Whitechapel murders but amongst the suspects, and to my mind a very likely one, was a Dr T. (which sounds much like D.) He was an American quack named Tumblety and was at one time a frequent visitor to London and on these occasions constantly brought under the notice of police, there being a large dossier concerning him at Scotland Yard. Although a 'Sycopathia Sexualis' subject he was not known as a 'Sadist' (which the murderer unquestionably was) but his feelings toward women were remarkable and bitter in the extreme, a fact on record. Tumblety was arrested at the time of the murders in connection with unnatural offences [according to Tumblety himself in an interview in the *New York World* of 29 January 1889, he was actually arrested in Whitechapel on suspicion of being Jack the Ripper] and charged at Marlborough Street, remanded on bail, jumped his bail, and got away to Boulogne.

Cover of the 'Kidnapping of Dr Tumblety'.
(*Stewart P. Evans*)

> He shortly left Boulogne and was never heard of afterwards. It was believed he committed
> suicide but certain it is that from this time the 'Ripper' murders came to an end.

In fact 'Dr' Francis Tumblety had not committed suicide, but having been arrested for an act of gross indecency with other men on 7 November 1888 he had jumped bail and fled to America under the assumed name Frank Townshend. Tumblety was an Irish-American quack doctor and braggart known to have a hatred of women; he was followed to the States by Inspector Andrews, who failed to locate him. A convincing suspect who fits the modern 'profile' of a serial killer, it is worthy of note that such killers often take trophies. The Ripper's second victim, Annie Chapman, was known to wear two brass rings – they were noted as missing when her body was found in the back yard of 29 Hanbury Street in 1888; when Tumblety finally died of a heart condition at St John's Hospital, St Louis in 1903, among his few effects were 'two imitation rings worth $3.'

It was not long before Jack the Ripper entered into folk legend as a popular bogeyman-like monster to frighten children if they misbehaved. Many a parent was known to threaten 'Jack the Ripper will get you!' Residents, those on business, and even casual visitors to London would often weave tall tales for fascinated young family members how *they* saw Jack the Ripper when they were in London during the autumn of 1888. These stories have been passed down generations and there are still a few households who can tell of how Great Aunt so-and-so or Great-Great Grandad saw Jack the Ripper flit among the shadows or run past them on the street complete with his top hat, sweeping cape, face partially obscured by an upturned collar, and eyes that 'burned like coals from hell itself.' In the quieter corners of the East End pubs there was many a tale told with hushed voices and narrowed eyes of how the huddled figure of Polly Nichols, emitting a ghoulish green glow, had been seen lying in the gutter of Buck's Row, and even how the horrible death-rattle and groans of Annie Chapman had been heard on old Hanbury Street. Jack the Ripper's legacy beyond the grave even extends to the skipping chant of East End children, and they state the only thing we can say for sure about Jack the Ripper today:

> Jack the Ripper's dead,
> And lying on his bed
> He cut his throat
> With Sunlight soap.
> Jack the Ripper's dead.

5

JACK'S BACK?

The Murder of Frances Coles, 1891

Early on Friday 13 February 1891, PC Ernest Thompson 240H, a young officer who had been on the force barely two months, was on his first solo night duty. Thompson had been on duty since 10 p.m. the previous night; his beat was to patrol Chamber Street and Prescott Street. He started from his point at the bottom of Chamber Street, patrolling up that street, and then along Prescott Street, passing small portions of Mansell and Leman Streets as he did so. There were three passageways formed by railway arches leading from Chamber Street to Royal Mint Street.

At about 2 a.m. Thompson was proceeding along Chamber Street from Leman Street. There was no one about, but when he was about 80 yards from the railway arch passageways opposite the Catholic Schools his attention was drawn by the sound of retreating footsteps, undoubtedly those of a man, travelling at a walking pace in the distance, apparently heading toward Mansell Street. As a good policeman he duly noted the steps and even looked at the clock on the top of the tower of the Co-operative Stores in Leman Street, noting it was very near 2.15 a.m., however, he did not consider them suspicious enough to pursue them. This was a decision Thompson would regret for the rest of his life.

Moments later Thompson went down a dingy, narrow passageway under one of the railway arches (with the misleadingly attractive name of Swallow Gardens) opposite the Catholic Schools in Chamber Street, Whitechapel. PC Thompson later deposed:

The roadway under the arch is partially taken away and boarded up from the crown of the arch to the ground. What remains is a roadway, enabling one cart to pass at a time. I should say the length of the arch is something over 40 yards. There are two ordinary street gas-lamps to light this arch, and they throw a light down the archway. I cannot tell the exact position of the light at the other entrance. If I was standing at the Chamber Street entrance to the archway I should be able to see anyone in the centre of the arch. I could see right through it; and I can do this at night. The centre part is not very light in the daytime … When I turned into the passage I could see a body lying under the arch on the roadway, about midway under the arch. I turned my lamp on as soon as I got there.

I could not see it was a woman until I turned my lamp on. I noticed some blood. I saw her open and shut one eye. I blew my whistle three times.

First on the scene was neighbouring Police Sergeant Hyde 161 H, who was about 250 yards away from the other end of the arch on Royal Mint Street when he heard the whistle and came running, closely followed by PC Hinton 275H, who had been on plain-clothes duty in front of Baron Rothschild's refinery [the names cited for the two police officers who responded to Thompson's whistle are those recorded in police report Ref. MEPO 3/140, ff.112-4; contemporary newspaper accounts however state their names as Police Constable Frederick Hart 161H and PC George Elliott 275H]. When Hyde arrived he turned on his police lamp, examined the woman, and found that her throat was cut. Telling Thompson to stay with the body, Hyde ran for Dr Oxley on Dock Street. Oxley was in bed but got up, dressed, and was at the murder scene in ten minutes, where he pronounced life extinct. Meanwhile, PC Hinton ran to Leman Street police station to report the matter to Inspector Flanagan, who in turn sent word to the Chief and Local Inspector and Dr George Bagster Phillips, the Divisional Surgeon, who soon arrived in a cab. Having ascertained to his satisfaction that life was extinct, Phillips made a minute examination of the body and the position in which it was lying and this was reported in *The Times*:

The woman was bareheaded, and her hair was disarranged, indicating that she had been engaged in some sort of struggle. One arm was stretched by her side, while the other was bent towards the breast. Close by the side of the dead woman was her hat, which was formed of very old crape. The deceased was then searched, when, to the surprise of the spectators, another hat was found in the folds of her dress. This article may, hereafter, have an important bearing on the case. In the pocket was found an old comb and a few pieces of cloth or rags, but no money. The latter fact caused the police to make a careful search round the place, with the result that a 2s piece was found. This probably shows the cause for which the victim was enticed to the spot where she met her end. The body was afterwards placed on an ambulance, and conveyed to the Leman Street police station, and afterwards to the Whitechapel mortuary.

In his report, Superintendent Tom Arnold noted:

The vicinity of Swallow Gardens was carefully searched, and in a space between a water pipe and some brickwork, about 18 yards from where the body was found Inspector Flanagan discovered 2s wrapped in two pieces of old newspaper, apparently *Daily News*, upon which there was no date. There is nothing to connect the money with the murder nor has any instrument or article been found likely to afford a clue.

At about 5 o'clock, Chief Inspector Donald S. Swanson arrived, accompanied by Inspector Moore, and took charge of the case. Having examined the spot where the body was found, Inspector Swanson gave orders that a portion of the blood should be

Right: The man who discovered the body of Frances Coles: PC Ernest Thompson 240H.

Below: The cover story of the Frances Coles murder from the *Penny Illustrated Paper*. (*Stewart P. Evans*)

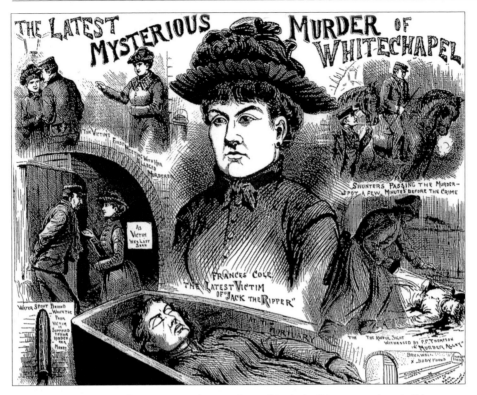

A connection between the Frances Coles murder and Jack the Ripper was irresistible to the press.

saved for the purpose of analysis, while the remainder was afterwards washed away. Later on the Chief Constable of the East End district, Melville Macnaghten (Chief Constable CID), Robert Anderson (Assistant Commissioner CID), and other leading police officials arrived at the scene to be appraised of the situation personally. With the news of another woman of the 'unfortunate' class being found with her throat cut on the streets of Whitechapel, the alarm bells were set ringing in the minds of these investigating officers, many of them veterans of the 1888 Jack the Ripper murders. News of another 'Jack the Ripper' murder was soon spreading across the force and the rest of London – the newspapers didn't need any prompting in this notion either.

Within the day a potential witness, William 'Jumbo' Friday, a carman in the employ of the Great Northern Railway, came forward to state he saw a man and woman in the shadows of a doorway near the entrance to Swallow Gardens at the Royal Mint Street end as he passed by at 1.45 a.m. He could not discern their faces, but noticed the woman wore a black hat – which, when shown the hat worn by the deceased, he identified as the one he had seen the woman wearing. He also gave a slight description of the man she was with but had to admit he did not see his face.

The deceased woman was known to police of H Division as a prostitute. She was formally identified as Frances Coles (26), but was known on the streets she had walked for about eight years as 'Carrotty Nell'. Over the last couple of days she had been spotted in the company of Tom Sadler (53), a fireman on the SS *Fez*. Sadler was rapidly tracked down by Detective Sergeant Don and PC Gill to the Phoenix public house in Upper East Smithfield on 14 February. He came quietly, saying, 'I expected this,' adding on the way to Leman Street police station,

> I am a married man and this will part me and my wife, you know what sailors are, I used her for my purpose for I have known Frances for some years. I admit I was with her, but I have a clean bill of health and can account for my time. I have not disguised myself in any way, and if you could not find me the detectives in London are no damned good.

Interviewed by Chief Inspector Swanson – and after confirming his name as James Thomas Sadler and stating his place of residence as Dann's Boarding House, East Smithfield – Sadler gave the following detailed statement:

> I am a fireman and am generally known as Tom Sadler. I was discharged at 7 p.m. on the 11th inst. from the steamship *Fez*. I think I had a drink of Holland's gin at Williams Brothers', at the corner of Goulston Street. I then went, at 8.30 p.m., to the Victoria Home. I then left the Home and went into the Princess Alice opposite, and had something to drink. I had no person with me. While in the Princess Alice, between 8.30 and 9 p.m., I saw a woman (whom I had previously known, named Frances). I had known her for 18 months. I first met her in the Whitechapel Road, and went with her to Thrawl Street, to a lodging-house, and I stayed with her all night; having paid for a double bed at the lodging-house. I don't remember the name of the lodging-house where I then stayed with her. I think I then took a ship, the name of which I do not remember.
>
> I did not see this woman again until I saw her in another bar of the Princess Alice, and recognising her, I beckoned her over to me. There was nobody with her. She asked me to leave the public house, as when she had got a little money the customers in the public house expected her to spend it amongst them. We left the Princess Alice, and went round drinking at other public houses. Among other houses I went into a house at the corner of Dorset Street, where another woman (named Annie Lawrence) joined us. Frances stopped me from treating this woman, and we then went to White's Row Chambers. I paid for a double bed, and we stayed the night there. She had a bottle of whisky (half-pint), which I had bought at Davis's, White Swan, Whitechapel. I took the bottle back yesterday morning, and the young woman (barmaid) gave me two-pennyworth of drink for it.
>
> Frances and I left White's Row Chambers between 11 and 12 noon, and we went into a number of public houses, one of which was the Bell, Middlesex Street. We stayed there for about two hours drinking and laughing. When in the Bell, she spoke to me about a hat which she had paid a shilling for a month previously. We then went on the way to the bonnet shop drinking at the public houses on the way. The shop is in White's Row or Baker's Row, and I gave her the half-a-crown which was due for the hat and she went into the shop. She came out again and said that her hat was not ready; the woman was putting some elastic on. We then went into a public house in White's or Baker's Row, and we had some more drinks. Then she went for her hat and got it; and brought it to me at

the public house, and I made her try it on. I wanted her to throw the old one away, but she declined, and I pinned it onto her dress. Then we went to the Marlborough Head public house, in Brick Lane, and had some more drink.

I was then getting into drink, and the landlady rather objected to Frances and me being in the house. I can't remember what the landlady said now. I treated some men in the house. I can't say their names. I had met them previously in the same house. From there I had an appointment to see a man Nichols in Spital Street, and I left her there to see Nichols, arranging to meet her again at a public house – where I cannot say now, and I have forgotten it. We came down Thrawl Street, and while going down a woman with a red shawl struck me on the head and I fell down, and when down I was kicked by some men around me. The men ran into the lodging-houses, and on getting up I found my money and my watch gone. I was then penniless, and I then had a row with Frances, for I thought she might have helped me when I was down. I then left her at the corner of Thrawl Street without making any appointment that I can remember.

I was downhearted at the loss of my money, because I could not pay for my bed. I then went to the London Docks and applied for admission, as I wanted to go aboard the steamship *Fez*. There was a stout sergeant inside the gate and a constable. They refused me admission, as I was too intoxicated. I cannot remember what hour this was, as I was dazed and drunk. There was a metropolitan police officer near the gate, a young man. I abused the sergeant and constable because they refused me admission. There were some dock labourers coming out, and they said something to me, and I replied abusively, and one of the labourers took it up, saying, 'If the policeman would turn his back he would give me a good hiding.' The policeman walked across the road, across Nightingale Lane, towards the Tower way, and as soon as he had done so the labourers made a dead set at me, especially the one who took my abuse. This one knocked me down and kicked me, and eventually another labourer stopped him. I then turned down Nightingale Lane and the labourers went up Smithfield way. I remained in Nightingale Lane for about a quarter of an hour, feeling my injuries.

I then went to the Victoria lodging house in East Smithfield, and applied for a bed, but was refused, as I was so drunk, by the night porter, a stout, fat man. I begged and prayed him to let me have a bed, but he refused. To the best of my belief I told him I had been knocked about. He refused to give me a bed, and I left and wandered about. I cannot say what the time was. I went towards Dorset Street: I cannot say which way, but possibly Leman Street way. When I got to Dorset Street I went into the lodging house where I had stopped with Frances on the previous night, and found her in the kitchen, sitting with her head on her arms. I spoke to Frances about her hat. She appeared half-dazed from drink, and I asked her if she had enough money to pay the double bed with. She said she had no money, and I told her I had not a farthing, but I had £4 15s coming to me. I asked her if she could get trust, but she said she could not. I then went to the deputy and asked for a night's lodging on the strength of the money I was to lift the next day, but I was refused. I was eventually turned out by a man, and left Frances behind in the house.

I then went, to the best of my belief, towards the London Hospital, and about the middle of the Whitechapel Road a young policeman stopped me and asked where I was going, as I looked in a pretty pickle. I said that I had had two doings last night, one in Spitalfields and one at the docks. I said I had been cut or hacked about with a knife or bottle. Immediately I mentioned the word knife he said, 'Oh, have you a knife about you?' and then searched me. I told him I did not carry a knife. My shipmates, one Mat Curley and another named Bowen, know that I have not carried a knife for years. The policeman helped me across the road towards the hospital gate. I spoke to the porter, but he hummed and hawed about it, and I began to abuse him. However, he did let me in, and I went to the accident ward and had the cut in my head dressed. The porter asked me if I had any place to go to, and I said no, and he let me lay down on a couch in the room where the first accidents are brought in. I can give no idea of the time I called at the hospital.

When he let me out, somewhere between 6 and 8 o'clock in the morning, I went straight to the Victoria Home, and begged for a few halfpence; but I did not succeed. I then went to the shipping office, where I was paid £4 15s 3d. Having got my money, I went to the Victoria, Upper East Smithfield, and stayed there all day, as I was miserable. The furthest I went out was the Phoenix, about twelve doors off. I spent the night there and I was there this morning. I had gone to the Phoenix this morning to have a drink, and I was beckoned out and asked to come here (Leman Street) and I came. As far as I can think, it was between 5 and 6 that I was assaulted in Thrawl Street at any rate it was getting dark, and it was some hours after that that I went to the London Docks. I forgot to mention that Frances and I had some food at Mr Shuttleworth's, in Wentworth-street.

My discharges are as follows: Last discharged 11-2-90 in London ship *Fez*. Next discharge 6-9-90, London. Next 15-7-90, London. Next 27-5-90, Barry. Next 1-10-89, London. Next 2-10-88, London. Engaged, 17-8-86; next, 5-5-87; engaged, 24-3-87, London. The last I had seen of the woman Frances was when I left her in the lodging-house when I was turned out. The lodging-house deputy can give you the name. The clothes that I am now wearing are the only clothes I have. They are the clothes I was discharged in and I have worn them ever since. My wife resides in the country, but I would prefer not to mention it. The lodging-house I refer to is White's Row, not Dorset Street. It has a large lamp over it. Passing a little huckster's shop at the corner of Brick Lane and Brown's Lane I purchased a pair of earrings, or rather I gave her the money and she bought them. I think she gave a penny for them.

This statement was read out on the second day of the inquest held before Mr Wynne E. Baxter, the East London coroner at the Working Lads' Institute, Whitechapel. The reading of the statement was followed by Divisional Surgeon George Bagster Phillips' detailed account of his post-mortem examination of the body:

On Saturday morning I made a minute examination of the incision in the throat. There was an external wound, the edges of the skin being not exactly cut through, there being a portion of about an inch long undivided. In my opinion, there were three distinct passings of the knife across the throat – one from left to right, one from right to left, and the third from left to right. Below the wound there was an abrasion, as if caused by a finger nail. Above the wound there were four abrasions, possibly caused by fingernails.

Tom Sadler and Frances Coles in the kitchen of the lodging house on White's Row.

From the position of these marks I opine that the left hand was used. There were some contused wounds on the back of the head, which I am of opinion were caused by the head coming into violent contact with paving stones. I came to the conclusion that death had been almost instantaneous, occasioned by the severance of the carotid arteries and other vessels on the left side. In my opinion, the deceased was on the ground when her throat was cut. I think that her assailant used his right hand in making the incisions in the throat, and that he had used his left hand to hold her head back by the chin; that he was on the right side of the body when he made the cuts. The tilting of the body to the left was to prevent the perpetrator from being stained with blood. There was a complete absence of any struggle or even any movement from pain, but it may have arisen from the fact that the woman was insensible from concussion. The knife produced would be capable of inflicting all the wounds found on the neck. It was not a very sharp knife that caused the wounds. On Monday, the 16th, I examined the sailor's cap produced.

Mortuary photograph of Frances Coles.
(*Stewart P. Evans*)

Tom Sadler in the dock at
Thames Police Court.

It was saturated with blood. The left and right cuffs of a shirt were stained with blood. The coat had two spots of blood on the right breast and two drops on the right sleeve. There was also a deposit of blood inside the right sleeve. The boots had no blood on them. On Monday, the 16th, I examined Sadler at Arbour Square police station. I found two wounds on the scalp, and the appearances of the blood on the clothes were consistent with its having come from either of these wounds.

Of course, modern forensics could have proved the matter conclusively, but in the late nineteenth century they were just developing the science of identifying the difference between mammalian and human blood – blood type or DNA did not enter into the equation. The inquest resumed, and what was to prove to be its final day of hearing was Friday 27 February 1891. More witnesses came forward placing Sadler and Coles in each others' company, something Sadler never denied, but the crucial placement of Sadler at the scene at the time of the murder proved impossible – there were simply no witnesses to do so. Wynne Baxter summed up at great length, placing all the facts adduced by the witnesses in review. The case, he said, had many characteristics in common with the murders which had preceded it; but it was for the jury to decide, taking well into consideration Sadler's drunken condition, the conflicting evidence as to times and the connected account given by him of his movements before and after the murder was committed, whether they could fairly charge him with the deed, or they must attribute it to some person or persons unknown.

The jury retired to consider their verdict. On their return, the foreman declared: 'We find that the deceased was wilfully murdered by some person or persons unknown, and we wish to say that we think the police did their duty in detaining Sadler.'

The police had made their enquiries; reading their reports they were sure they had the right man but simply did not have witnesses, evidence, murder weapon or forensics to provide proof of his guilt. The lack of mutilation and the method of throat cutting does not evince this as a Jack the Ripper crime – even if he was interrupted – but it is true to say that many officers involved in the case, particularly the beat policemen, really did believe they were on the trail of Jack the Ripper. Tales of their exploits have no doubt entered family legend over the years – and to be honest, we can never know with absolute certainty that they were not correct in their assumption.

As a postscript it may be of interest to note that the murder of Frances Coles is the last case included in the extant police and Home Office files concerning the Jack the Ripper murders. These records continue to 1892/3, where they record a complaint of assault and threats to kill made by Sadler against his wife Sarah. So acute was her fear that she was 'afraid to live with him any longer.' Both Mrs Sadler and her lodger, Naval pensioner Mr Moffatt, describe Sadler, curiously, as 'a most violent, subtle and treacherous man.' The final report in the file records Sadler was bound on his recognisance to keep the peace towards his wife for six months 'and the wife appears to desire that he should still remain under some surveillance.'

6

THE WHITECHAPEL NEWSPAPER SHOP MURDER

Conrad Donovan & Charles Wade, 1904

Miss Matilda Emily Farmer lived a quiet life running her small newsagent and tobacconist shop, which she lived above at 478 Commercial Road, Whitechapel. She was 63 years old, but looked younger. She was also considered by some to be rather eccentric because she would never allow anyone but family into the upstairs portion of her house; coupled with her usual neat appearance and habit of wearing gold pince-nez, three gold rings (one with four diamonds) on one finger, two bracelets and a gold watch chain around her neck, it was rumoured she 'had money', and because she did not allow anyone upstairs it was thought by some that she probably kept a large sum of money on the premises. Miss Farmer was also a creature of habit. You could almost set your watch by her routine of going down into her shop every morning between 5.45 a.m. and 6 a.m. to receive the boy who delivered the daily newspapers, after which she would see to it they were all neatly folded and ready for distribution to her customers; then she would go into the parlour at the back of the shop where she would prepare and eat her breakfast. At about 6.30 a.m. Harry Wiggins (11), the errand boy, would arrive and take down the shop shutters and then busy himself delivering the newspapers.

The morning of Wednesday 12 October 1904 began a little misty and the chill touched the boy who brought the papers to Miss Farmer. By the time Wiggins arrived at 6.30 a.m. the day was already brightening, but there was no sign of Miss Farmer. He carried on with his tasks and served customers until about 7.30 a.m. – when he noticed her false teeth, a soda-water bottle and tumbler on the floor. He mentioned what he had seen, and raised his concerns about Miss Farmer not being around, to another lad, who told Miss Baker, a neighbouring shopkeeper – who in turn brought the matter to the attention of a policeman (PC 141H). Upon investigation the officer found the false teeth and a boot on the floor of the shop near the counter. Passing through the counter area and proceeding up the stairs, he found a broken portion of a pair of spectacles. He was followed by Miss Baker.

The police officer's worst fears were confirmed as he entered the upstairs front room, where he discovered the body of Miss Farmer lying at the foot of her bed. Her hands had been tied behind her back and she had been gagged with a towel forced into her mouth and tied in place with another cloth. The constable immediately removed the gag, and cut her hands free, while Miss Baker helped him lay her on the bed and unfasten her dress and corsets. Miss Baker and the constable felt Miss Farmer's heart and believed they felt a faint heartbeat. The Divisional Surgeon, Dr Charles Graham Grant, who lived almost opposite the shop, was rapidly summoned to the scene, but Miss Farmer's heart had stopped before he got there and immediately upon his initial examination he declared life extinct. (At the trial, Dr Grant stated he did not think Miss Farmer was alive when the police officer thought he felt her heartbeat: for anyone without formal medical training such a mistake was a 'common thing'. This view was endorsed by Mr Pepper, the surgeon called as an expert witness at the trial.) Further examination revealed that more than one person must have been involved in tying Miss Farmer's hands behind her back. She had suffocated as a result of the gag forced into her mouth. From the appearance of the body, there had not been a struggle.

Soon on the scene were Superintendent J. Mulvaney, Detective Inspector T. Divall, Sub-Divisional Inspector A. Holland and Detective Sergeant Wensley. They too agreed Miss Farmer had died without a struggle, but the jewellery she was known to wear was missing, as was a small tin she used for her takings. Her drawers had been tipped out over the floor and it was clear the room had been ransacked as the robbers searched for further hidden money or valuables.

As soon as the papers filled with news of this crime, a man walked into a police station at Worthing. His name was James Pitzpatrick (31), a billiard marker of no fixed abode, and he confessed to the crime, giving a full statement to Sergeant Dean. It might seem like an open-and-shut case, but any experienced police officer will tell you, even today, that once a murder gets media coverage, the false confessions will start coming in. When Fitzpatrick's statement was compared to the facts known to the police (and a short investigation of Fitzpatrick's whereabouts on the dates in question revealed he had been admitted to the Brighton Infirmary on 10 October and only discharged at 8 a.m. on the morning of the murder), the police knew he was lying. Fitzpatrick was brought before Thames Magistrates, where he formally retracted his confession, claiming, 'I was destitute and wished to get back at my friends at Whitechapel.' Perhaps the homeless man was hoping to get accommodation courtesy of Her Majesty through the cold winter for making a false statement, but no such quarter was given and Mr Mead, the magistrate, discharged Fitzpatrick.

The detectives, however, were not quite back to square one as a genuine key witness had came forward, namely Robert Rae (18), a fishmonger of Old Church Road, Stepney. He had known a certain Conrad Donovan (34) (real name Joseph

Potten or Potter) when Donovan lived almost opposite where Rae worked. Rae had not seen Donovan for a while, but on the morning of 12 October, after being on night work, he stopped at Gosling's Coffee Shop on Commercial Road (where he stayed for about ten minutes) before walking up the road to Miss Farmer's shop (which was almost opposite Old Church Road), arriving there about 6.30 a.m. A man Rae had seen with Donovan in the past (later identified as Charles Wade (22), Donovan's half-brother) came out of Farmer's (apparently closed) shop with a newspaper in his hand, closely followed by Donovan, who also had a newspaper in his hands. Rae thought it curious that both men hurried out of the shop leaving the door open. He also noticed there was no light on inside.

Donovan and Wade then strolled on across the road and stopped, Donovan apparently pointing something out to Wade in the paper, but Rae did not hear them speak. The two men then walked as far as Stepney Temple, where they stopped again for a few seconds. Donovan then made some motion with his hands and they walked on again in the direction of Poplar. A short while later, Rae saw the shop boy arrive and begin to take the shutters off – no one had gone in or out of the shop in the meantime.

Rae was concerned: he met a couple of acquaintances on his way home and mentioned what he had seen, but he was tired after his long shift and, as he stated at the inquest, he feared violent repercussions from Donovan or his associates if he reported his concerns of a robbery to the police. Instead, he went home to bed. Rae woke again at 10 a.m., when he learned from his mother (with whom he lived) that there had, in fact, been a murder in the newspaper shop on Commerical Road. Rae immediately told her what he had seen and the following day Detective Inspector Divall and Sergeant Wensley called to see him to take his statement. By the following Sunday the police had successfully tracked down and apprehended Donovan and Wade (arrested on 16 October) and Rae was brought to Arbour Square police station, where he successfully picked out both suspects from a line-up of twelve men.

Conrad Donovan, who gave his occupation as a sailor of Church Road, Limehouse, and his half-brother Charles Wade, a labourer residing at Grosvenor Street, Ratcliff, were charged on remand at Thames Police Court on Tuesday 25 October 1904. Wade and Donovan were brought before Mr Justice Grantham at the Central Criminal Court on 18 November 1904. Mr Charles Matthews and Mr Arthur Gill acted for the prosecution and Mr Percival Hughes, Mr Paul Methven and Mr Gathorne Harvey for the defence. In the light of the evidence presented so far – and with a Mr Richard Barnes (26), a painter residing in Stepney Causeway, coming forward to say that he saw Wade with 'another man' (both of whom he identified in a line up with twelve other men at Brixton Prison) crossing Commercial Road on the morning of the murder, heading in the direction of Miss Farmer's shop) – the defence were going to have a thankless task. After a few questions examining the state of the witnesses' eyesight and the light on the morning in question, they could do little to damage the credibility of the witnesses.

On the second day of the trial Barnes continued his testimony, revealing he had also seen Wade on the night before the murder. Between 10 p.m. and 11 p.m. on 11 October, Barnes had been coming out of Stepney Causeway towards Dorset Street when he saw Wade and another man (whom he identified as Donovan) talking 'about 6 yards from Miss Farmer's shop.' On the morning of the murder Barnes was on his way to a coffee shop on Commercial Road when he spotted Wade and Donovan crossing the road. He recalled arriving at the coffee shop at about 6.03 a.m. After about three quarters of an hour he left the coffee shop, went home and then proceeded to the Friend's Institute at the corner of Dorset Street, where he was working. Shortly before he arrived at the institute, just before 8 a.m., he passed Miss Farmer's shop and saw a group of people outside the shop and a policeman going inside. Within minutes he heard the news that Miss Farmer had been murdered. It didn't take much to put two and two together: Donovan and Wade were both known as violent men in their own right. Barnes 'thought it was an extraordinary thing to see Wade standing in Commercial Road in the morning after seeing him there on the night before.'

When asked why he had not come forward sooner, it transpired that – like Rae – Barnes was also afraid of possible reprisals. He stated he was 'forbidden by his parents to say anything.' His mother was suffering from heart disease and she forbade him to say anything about it, 'because his father was robbed and beaten three years ago in Dorset Street and she was afraid that persons would do it again as it was such a rough neighbourhood.' however, realising how important his testimony would be (and being a Sunday school teacher), despite his parent's fears, he finally decided to come forward.

On 21 November, the final day of the hearing, Mr Matthews for the prosecution summed up the facts and admitted that none of the stolen goods were found in the possession of the accused. Though this was an important point for the defence, the men, he said, could easily have got rid of the stolen goods and, most importantly, the witnesses placed both men at the scene at the relevant times. Percival Hughes for the defence delivered his address to the jury over several hours and suggested the evidence against the accused was weak. He contended the prosecution had failed to prove that Donovan and Wade were the persons who committed the crime – and questioned the positive identification of the accused by the witnesses by alluding to and attempting to capitalise on the recent case of Adolf Beck. Beck had been arrested, tried and convicted after female victims of fraud wrongly identified him in the street as the perpetrator. When the real guilty party, another man named Wilhelm Meyer – who bore a remarkable likeness to Beck – was caught for 'Beck'-style frauds, the case was blown open. Beck was finally pardoned and freed with compensation on 27 July 1904.

The question of identity and the relevance of the Beck case were also dealt with by Mr Justice Grantham in his summing up. He qualified his satisfaction with the standard of testimony: 'In this case it was a very different class of evidence, as the witnesses who had identified the prisoners were persons who had known them.'

The jury then retired to deliberate, and after only ten minutes returned a verdict of 'guilty' against both prisoners. When asked by the Clerk of Arraigns if they had anything to say as to why sentence of death should not be passed upon them, Donovan and Wade made no reply.

Justice Grantham donned the black cap; before he passed sentence he commented that he was not surprised the prisoners were in this situation, knowing something as he did of their lives – both had previous convictions and had served custodial sentences for violence and robbery. He expressed sadness that Wade, the younger man, had been corrupted by Donovan, but none the less concluded, 'It was a fortunate thing for society that the persons had been caught and were going to meet the doom for the crime of which they had been convicted, and which was committed for the sake of gain.' His lordship then passed the death sentence upon both men, who both received it with 'utmost sangfroid.'

As the prisoners were taken down, someone in the public gallery shouted, 'Cheer up!' Wade managed to lean over the dock and, after issuing an expletive, snarled at one of the detectives, 'If I could get at you I would settle you in two seconds.' The prisoners were then removed from the dock and taken to Pentonville Prison.

Just eight days before the pair were due to hang, workmen repairing the house where the murder was committed found Miss Farmer's jewellery under some floorboards. Questions were raised, but in the final analysis this discovery only gave another reason why the police failed to discover any of the stolen property on Donovan or Wade – they simply had not got away with it in the first place.

On Tuesday 13 December 1904, executioner William Billington, assisted by Henry Pierrepoint (father of Albert Pierrepoint), executed Donovan and Wade. In an official announcement by the Under-Sheriff, Mr F.K. Metcalfe, death, in both cases, was recorded as 'Instantaneous.' Wade left no final words, but in a statement to the prison chaplain, Donovan said, 'No murder was intended.'

7

BLOOD ON THE STREETS

The Tottenham Outrage, the Houndsditch Murders
& the Siege of Sydney Street

The East End of London has always been a refuge for immigrants, some of them genuinely fleeing oppression or persecution because of their race or creed, while others use this cover to flee the law. Quite how (or if) all three of the following cases were *really* connected may never be discovered, but the press in the early twentieth century seemed set on finding a link between them and popular fears about anarchist plots to overthrow law and order and government, and perhaps, dared they even moot, a threat to our own monarchy – at least they gave column space to publish the letters of those who would suggest such fears. Some were blatantly xenophobic.

All we can say with some certainty is that all of those involved in these crimes were immigrants from Central Europe, while some certainly had criminal records in the countries they had fled from and quite probably saw the anarchist movements as a vehicle for their criminal plans; some had strong political beliefs, and there appeared to be a core of Lithuanian men and women involved in the crimes who had banded together to form the 'Leesma' or 'Flame' group of Lettish anarchists, who allied themselves with Lettish Socialistic Revolutionary Party – though it must be said that all revolutionary parties vehemently distanced themselves from these criminal actions. Above all, those who carried out the crimes were armed with pistols and copious amounts of ammunition and were not afraid of using them. For the first time serious armed pursuits – using what were, in those days, modern vehicles and weaponry – took place in the capital and blood ran on the streets.

Our story begins in Tottenham, north-east London, on Saturday 23 January 1909, and a failed attempt at a wages snatch at Schnurmann's rubber factory on Chestnut Road. Just across the road from the factory was Tottenham police station and when shots were heard the police ran to investigate. Despite struggling with the robbers and being fired upon at close range, by some miracle, Albert Keyworth (17), the office boy who carried the wages, and Joseph Wilson (29), the chauffeur who drove the boy to and from the bank, were uninjured, though the driver's coat was peppered with shot and a bullet grazed across his stomach, which cut through everything – including his vest – save the man himself.

The two robbers, having successfully wrestled away the wages bag, ran from the scene down Chestnut Road. Police were soon in hot pursuit, with more off-duty officers joining in, piling out of the nearby section house. Passers-by pointed them in the direction of the fleeing robbers: some even bravely ran after them. George Smith, a burly stoker, brought one of the men down with a flying tackle. The other man pointed the gun at Smith, firing four times at his head. Smith was also incredibly lucky: the shots grazed his scalp, and another caught him on the flesh of his collar bone. Smith was pushed off and the robbers picked up the wages sack again and took to their heels, with police officers now closing in on them. The men ran through terraced streets, fending off police officers with shots from their pistols if they got too close.

One of the gunmen stopped near the Mission Hall on Mitchley Road to reload. As he did so the factory car driven by brave chauffer Wilson swung into the road. With him was PC Newman 510N, and running alongside were the factory manager and PC Tyler 403N. PC Newman told Wilson to run down the gunman if he could. As the car accelerated towards the gunmen they coldly took aim and fired simultaneously – Newman was torn across the cheek and ear as the car windscreen shattered under the hail of bullets, while Wilson was cut across his neck and collar. Another shot burst the car's water pipe. Tragically, at the moment the gunmen fired, a ten-year-old boy, Ralph Joscelyne, ran into the road and was caught in the crossfire. Grievously wounded, he was taken to hospital, but was declared dead on arrival.

By this time word had been sent back to the police station to draw firearms. They had never been needed before and nobody knew where the key to the cabinet where they were kept was! The lock was smashed, weapons drawn, ammunition issued and the officers thrust the weaponry into the pockets of their tunics and set off in pursuit on bicycles.

The gunmen were now on Down Road, running towards the marshes by the River Lea. The indefatigable PCs Tyler and Newman, with PC Bond, knew the area well and took a shortcut in an attempt to head off the gunmen at the railway footbridge. PC Tyler was about 20 yards behind the men; he shouted, 'Come on, give in, the game's up!' One of the men (later identified as Paul Hefeld) turned and fired his Bergmann automatic pistol. PC Tyler's head rocked from the force of the bullet's impact and he fell, face down, onto the ground. He had been shot through the right side of his neck and was mortally wounded. The officers with him did what they could; they carried their fallen comrade to a nearby cottage where he died a short while later.

The gunmen ran on, crossing over Stonebridge Lock where they caught their breath, fending off their pursuers with pistol shots. Workmen saw the gunmen and ran over, facing more bullets which wounded a number of them. At a bridge the gunmen stopped again and held back their pursuers with more shots. Another police officer

With a revolver pressed to his head, tram conductor Charles Wyatt is ordered to drive the hijacked tram.

managed to get within range, only to find his gun was faulty – he was wounded in the calf and thigh before he could get back. The men ran on by the Banbury Reservoir. A policeman spotted a party shooting for duck and called for them to shoot at the gunmen. This unusual request took a while to sink in but when it did the sportsmen fired through the hedges at the gunmen, one of them appeared to react as if shot (his cap was later found peppered with shot) but he ran on.

After crossing more fields, even firing at a gypsy encampment, the two gunmen arrived at Salisbury Hall Farm where they spotted a tram. The tram driver, Joseph Slow, had seen the crowd, heard the cries of 'Murder!' and slowed down. Suddenly, one of the gunmen leapt out of a hedge and onto the platform of the tram. He ordered the driver to stop: the brakes were applied, and the other gunman caught up and jumped aboard. The pursuers – police, duck shooters and all – opened fire, shattering the tram windows and causing the passengers to fling themselves onto the floor; the driver fleeing to the upper deck. Seeing he had gone but not knowing where, one of the gunmen ordered the trapped conductor, Charles Wyatt, to drive the tram. The unfortunate conductor had never driven a tram, but with a gun pressed to his head was left with little option. He managed to get the tram to move off, and they left their pursuers behind.

A little way on, the tram passed another, which, when it went further up the road, was commandeered and put in reverse by the pursuers. A horse-drawn advertising cart had also been commandeered by armed policemen and was gaining on the gunmen's tram. One of the gunmen carefully took aim and shot the pony through the head, causing the cart to spill its occupants all over the road.

There had been only a few passengers on the tram when it was seized and most had managed to jump off in the confusion, but one man, Edward Loveday (63), was not agile enough to get away quickly. Agitated by the events, at Kite's Corner the old man appeared to make an attempt to snatch one of the gunmen's weapons: we will never know his true intention, as he was met by a shot in the throat. As the old man slumped dying to the floor, the desperate gunman leapt from the tram and went to take a milk cart. Mr Conyard the milkman came running over, but was instantly shot and wounded in the chest and arm. The gunmen got aboard the cart, whipped up the pony and drove hell for leather down Kenilworth Avenue, in the direction of Forest Road. Still managing to fire a few shots at their pursuers, PC Zeithing was shot through his coat, and PC Rushbrooke's bicycle was damaged during the pursuit. The gunmen turned this cart over at speed on a corner, but jumped clear and ran to Forest Road, where they forced a roundsman off the greengrocer's van he was driving at gunpoint, and, whipping this horse up, off they went again. The police then commandeered a chauffer-driven car and kept up the pursuit.

The gunmen probably wondered why they were not making the ground they desired as the cart struggled to make speed. It seems they had not realised the van's chain brake was still on. On Winchester Road they abandoned the van and ran off on foot towards the Ching Brook. In their haste they chose badly and ran along a footpath that converged with a wooden fence. They were trapped. One of the men was unable to go on: he could not manage the climb and fell back over the palings. He called to his accomplice to save himself and, grasping his pistol for the last time, placed the end of the barrel against his head and fired. The bullet entered about half an inch above the right eye and exploded out through the forehead on the other side. When the police arrived he was still alive and able to struggle violently as the police removed him, drenched in blood, to the Prince of Wales Hospital – where he died, two weeks later, on 12 February.

The remaining gunman ran through Beech Hall Estate, across Oak Hill, and then across fields to Oak Cottage at Hale End, on the edge of Epping Forest. Mrs Eliza Rolstone, who lived at Oak Cottage with her husband Charles and young family, had heard the police whistles and had hurried to her gate with her eldest child to see what was occurring. A policeman ran up to her and ordered her to, 'Go in and shut your door. There is a murderer about.' Mr Rolstone, a coal man, was at work and her younger children, aged 6 and 2, were inside at the table, so she hastened back up her path – but to her horror, she saw a man inside looking out at her. She ran into the field screaming, 'My children! My children!'

The gunman had bolted the front and back door. He paused for a drink from a mug on a table in front of the children before panicking and trying to climb up and hide in the parlour chimney. Failing in this attempt, he then fled upstairs. The man risked a glance out of the window, but was instantly spotted and greeted by a volley of shots from the pursuers that now surrounded the cottage, which shattered the window and wrecked much of the room inside. Seeing the gunman had gone upstairs, PC Dewhurst and Walthamstow baker Charles Schaffer, who had both been involved in the pursuit, seized their opportunity, smashed a window and got the children out. The building was surrounded.

PC Eagles borrowed a double-barrelled shotgun from a bystander and went into the scullery; hearing a noise upstairs he went outside to look for a ladder. Detectives Dixon and Cater got in through the ground-floor window. They saw sooty handprints on the wall and wondered if the man had climbed up the chimney to hide. Firing a shot up the chimney simply brought more soot down – he must be upstairs. Dixon crept up the stairs and, gaining the landing, cautiously opened the front bedroom door. In an instant he saw the gunman – and fired. Dixon shouted to the man to throw out his gun and give himself up. The gunman muttered he would not.

Meanwhile, PC Eagles had got his ladder from a neighbouring garden. He got into position and had the gunman in his sights. He pulled the trigger – and nothing happened. He quickly slid down the ladder again; there was no replying shot. What had seemed a never-ending supply of ammunition was now critically low: the gunman had just two shots left.

The detectives began to fire through the bedroom door – through the holes they saw the gunman wildly flinging himself around the walls. When PC Eagles arrived he begged a pistol from Detective Dixon, found the bedroom door open, but not wide, thrust his arm through and fired. The gunman taunted 'Come on now' as Eagles barged into the room, and both men fired – the gunman at himself. He fell back, shot in the head. The police officers dragged the gunman out into the yard. He took some time to die but as he did, all who saw him would be haunted by the sick grin he held across his face.

The chase had lasted over two hours and spread over six miles. Both gunmen had been using modern automatic pistols and it was reckoned that they had fired some 400 rounds of ammunition between them. Behind them they left a little boy, an elderly man and a policeman dead and about twenty-five people wounded by gunfire or injured as a direct result of the pursuit. For their bravery in the pursuit of the armed robbers, PC Eagles and Detectives Dixon and Carter were all promoted to Sergeant and were awarded the newly instituted King's Police Medal for Gallantry. PC Tyler was given a funeral with full honours which passed along streets many deep in spectators, estimated to be as many as 500,000 in number, along the route from Tyler's home on Arnold Road to Abney Park cemetery – where he was buried underneath a magnificent monument erected by the officers and men of the Metropolitan Police. Under a stone canopy, carved with remarkable detail, it shows his police helmet on top of his folded uniform.

At the same time Ralph Joscelyne was buried just a short distance away. His grave was marked by a fine stone cross erected by his fellow scholars at Earlsmead School and a plaque was erected to his memory in Child's Hill church. Ralph's mother,

The Rolstone's cottage at Hale End: the bedroom where Jacob Lapidus died is marked with an 'X'.

Mrs Louise Joscelyne, brought up seven other children but never recovered from the loss of her son, and when she died in 1952 the shoes the boy had been wearing when he was shot were buried with her.

Investigations soon revealed the gunmen were Paul Hefeld (nicknamed 'elephant') and Jacob Lapidus. Hefeld, who had attempted to take his own life after failing to climb the fence, spent most of his waking hours under police guard, glaring around the hospital ward to the degree that one officer recalled 'the look in his eyes seemed so full of hate, I was in no doubt if he could move he would not give a second thought to killing the lot of us.' Despite questions being put to him, Hefeld's only comment from the time of his capture was 'My mother is in Riga.' The other gunman, Jacob Lapidus (also recorded as Lepidus, though this surname – whichever spelling you choose – is thought to have been false), killed himself in the children's bedroom in the cottage at Hale End.

Both were political refugees from Latvia and soon the word on the street and in the press was that these desperate men were no ordinary robbers but anarchists and part of a conspiracy to overthrow British society. The *Daily Mirror* even went so far as to claim that Hefeld was the emissary of the Anarchist Secret Service Corps. Across London, but particularly in the East End, suspicion and xenophobia against immigrants, particularly Russians, intensified.

Almost two years later, the fears over anarchists were still grumbling on the street: and in the press if they had nothing better to print. Late on the night of 16 December 1910 it was blowing a gale and very few people braved the streets of Houndsditch. Max Weil, the owner of a fancy goods shop which adjoined H.S. Harris, Jewellers of 119 Houndsditch, had become concerned about noises which sounded like building works coming from the back of the shop, and, fearing someone was attempting to break in through the wall he sought out a constable. Finding City PC Walter Piper in Bishopgate, he brought the matter to his attention. Investigating the properties that adjoined the jeweller's, one man's furtive behaviour at 11 Exchange Buildings aroused Piper's suspicions – he had opened the door too quickly and clearly just wanted to get rid of the policeman (this man was later identified as George Gardstein). Piper also spotted another man lurking in the shadows nearby, who walked off as Piper approached. Something simply was not right.

Piper left the area and found two other officers from adjoining beats – PCs Walter Choat and Ernest Woodhams – who he guided to the shop, left them observing, and went to Bishopgate police station to summon more help. On his way there Piper encountered Robert Bentley, one of his duty sergeants, and two plain-clothed constables – James Martin and Arthur Strongman – who proceeded to the scene.

Soon the station had been alerted to the suspected burglary attempt, Mr Harris the jeweller had been called by the Night Duty Inspector to come and open his shop, and Sergeants Tucker and Bryant and PC Smoothey were despatched. Intelligence had been received that a 'suspicious group of foreigners' were living in the building adjoining the jeweller's where the noises were coming from.

At approximately 11.30 p.m. Sergeant Bentley, a brave ex-Dragoon, went to the door of 11 Exchange Buildings and knocked. Again, the suspicious man encountered by PC Piper yanked open the door. Bentley enquired, 'Have you been working or knocking about inside?' Gardstein said nothing. Bentley, losing patience, pressed, 'Don't you understand English?' Still there was no reply. Bentley was not going to give up. 'Have you got anybody in the house that can?' he asked. 'Fetch them down.'

Gardstein pushed the door closed a little and went upstairs. Still nothing was forthcoming so Sergeant Bentley pushed open the door and went inside, followed by Sergeant Bryant. Upon entering, the sergeants noticed three cups and saucers on a table. A man stood on the stairs inside: just his feet and the bottom of his trouser legs were visible. Bentley asked if they could look out the back and was directed by the man on the stairs with the words 'in there.' As Bentley crossed the room the back door burst open and a man walked briskly into the room. In his hand, at the end of his raised arm, was a pistol – and he had no compulsion about pulling the trigger. As he fired, so too did the man on the stairs. The first shots dazed more than damaged Bentley, but before he had time to recover himself the man from the door had walked to just the other side of the table and emptied two shots into Bentley at point blank range, one of which almost severed his spinal cord.

Bentley reeled back and collapsed on the doorstep. Bryant saw the pistols turn on him, and more shots rang out: he instinctively raised his hands against the flashes, felt his left hand fall to his side and blundered towards the door. Stumbling over the dying Bentley, he fled onto the street. Only then did he fully realise he had been shot in the arm and wounded in the chest. PC Woodhams was outside and ran over to assist Sergeant Bentley – but as he did so, a bullet cracked into his leg, shattering his femur. He fell to the ground.

Another man then ran out of the door firing a pistol. In the line of fire were Sergeant Tucker and PC Strongman. In an instant, Tucker was staggering and Strongman caught hold of him. Tucker managed to walk a few paces before he collapsed to the ground. He had been shot in the hip and the heart.

Soon a hail of fire opened up from the premises and the gang made a break for it, running towards the entrance of the Exchange Building's cul-de-sac which led onto Cutler Street. Here gang leader Gardstein had almost reached the exit when PC Choat grabbed hold of him and wrestled for the gun. Gardstein kept firing and Choat was shot in the leg. Other members of the gang then turned their guns on Choat: he was a big, strong policeman and used to handling himself on the streets, but with multiple bullet wounds, two of them in his back, he could fight no more and collapsed to the ground, dragging Gardstein with him. As he did so a bullet fired by the gang member and intended for Choat went into Gardstein's back. He was bleeding profusely and mortally wounded, but even then Choat would not release his grip on Gardstein. Choat was kicked in the face to make him let go, and the wounded Gardstein was bundled off into the darkness by fellow gang members.

The unarmed police were kept back by the blazing pistols of the gang and they got away into the night. Sergeant Bentley was removed to St Bartholomew's Hospital, where he died the following morning. Sergeant Tucker was pronounced dead on arrival at the London Hospital. He was followed by PC Choat, who, despite suffering a total of eight bullet wounds, was still conscious and underwent surgery. Removed to a ward, he died on 17 December. Gardstein lingered on but he was not to survive his wound either.

Dr John Scanlon had been called to attend a man suffering a bullet wound at 59 Grove Street. Upon examination the wound clearly showed it could not have been self-inflicted, and he informed the police. By the time Detective Inspector Wensley and Detective Sergeant Ben Leeson reached Grove Street, Gardstein was dead. Many clues were found in this squalid room: almost 100 rounds of assorted ammunition, a loaded Dreyse pistol under the pillow, bomb-making instructions and a pocket book containing Gardstein's membership card for the Lettish Anarchist Communist Group 'Leesma'. A representative meeting of the London groups of the Russian Revolutionary parties was quick to emphatically protest against any attempt on the part of the press or the police to link the 'anarchist' crimes to them, especially the recent Houndsditch Murders, and pointed out: 'The London Congress of 1907 expressly forbids any participation whatever in deeds of expropriation and this resolution has been carried out to the letter.'

The detective force had a massive task on their hands to identify and track down the other gang members. Informers were pressed to find out what they could, detectives worked round the clock following up leads, wanted posters were published and descriptions of those wanted circulated to police across London.

Nicholas Tomacoff, a young Russian musician, was caught by police as he visited 59 Grove Street. He swore he was only a friend of Fritz Svaars and that they were working on a Christmas play together for the Anarchist Club. When police apprised him of the situation, Tomacoff revealed the names of others he had seen at the address. A number of those believed to have been involved were soon in police custody – namely Osip Federoff and Luba Millstein. It was assumed Luba was the woman sought by the police but, although she was implicated, the woman the police really wanted (and who was described on the posters) was Nina Vassilleva. She was brought in and questioned but later released and observed in the hope she would lead the police to other gang members. On 22 December, Tomacoff led police to the men who carried Gardstein from the scene of the Houndsditch Murders – Jacob Peters and Yourka Dubof.

On the same day a poster showing a photo of Gardstein (an image created by making his corpse presentable and 'life like' in the mortuary) offering a £500 reward for information on his known accomplices – Fritz Svaars, a man known only as 'Peter the Painter' and an unnamed woman of whom police only had a description and no name – was supplied.

The wanted poster issued for Gardstein's accomplices in the Houndsditch Murders.

Inspector Wensley relating how
Sergeant Leeson was shot, at the
coroner's enquiry into the Siege of
Sidney Street.

From this appeal a man came forward who recognised Gardstein as his lodger at 44 Gold Street. What the police discovered there was described in the press as 'The Stepney Bomb Factory', reported to include 'materials suitable for the manufacture of bombs, a supply of deadly acids, cartridges sufficient to kill crowds and a quantity of anarchist literature.'

The break the police had been waiting for came on the bitterly cold evening of 1 January 1911. Charles Perelman, who had been the gang's original landlord when they took rooms at Great Garden Street and Wellesley Street, came forward with information that gang member William Sokolow, known to most simply as 'Joseph', had an association with a Mrs Betty Gershon and that since the Houndsditch Murders Joseph and Fritz Svaars and had been hiding out in Gershon's room at No. 100 Sidney Street.

Detective Inspector Wensley was not going to lose a moment; despite the driving gusts of sleet and snow all officers at his disposal were mobilized and despatched *post haste* to Sidney Street – the seriousness of the situation was reflected by the order that no married officers were required.

At 2.30 a.m. the first police contingent arrived at Sidney Street – a typical East London street of shops, pubs and houses between Mile End Road and Commercial Road. The building believed to harbour the suspects was one of a block of four-storey, red-brick houses built in 1900. By 3 a.m. over 200 officers were deployed, No. 100 Sidney Street was sealed off and adjacent buildings evacuated. The police officers then investigated No. 100. Gaining access via the landlord and landlady, the police soon found Mrs Gershon, who had been asleep in a stock room, dressed only in her petticoat – she explained the men had refused to leave and had made her take off her skirt and boots so she could not run away. She was removed to City Police headquarters.

The room containing the gang members was very difficult to access. Superintendent Mulvaney recorded:

> The measurements of the passage and staircase (staircase was 3½ft wide) will show how futile any attempt to storm or rush the place would have been… The passage at one discharge would have been blocked by fallen men; had any even reached the stairs, it could only have been by climbing over the bodies of their comrades… had they even done this the two desperadoes could retreat up the staircase to the first and second story, on each of which, what had occurred below would have been repeated.

There was also the problem that, by law, the police could not open fire on the room unless they had been fired upon first.

With a rush of the room out of the question the decision was taken to evacuate No. 100 Sidney Street; police snipers were placed in the buildings opposite and they waited for the dawn. As news got out of the police action, curious locals began to cluster against the police cordons. Shortly after 7.30 a.m., as the early morning light began to fill the grey sky and the sleet had turned to rain, the police decided to attract the attention of their quarry. Stationing themselves opposite No. 100 Sidney Street, in an alley which led to a wood yard, Sergeant Weston ran across the road to hammer on the still open door of No. 100 and then ran back again. Wensley then ordered stones to be thrown at the second-floor windows. Still there was no reaction. Then a copper picked up a brick and threw it, smashing a pane of glass – that did the trick. Half a dozen shots rang out at the police officers in the alley – one shot went through one of the detectives' bowler hats, but unfortunately, Sergeantt Ben Leeson was hit in the chest by another. The policemen retreated with their injured comrade to the wood yard. His wound was thought to be serious – indeed Leeson thought it a mortal wound – and as he lay on the floor tended by his colleagues, he said: 'Mr Wensley, I am dying. They have shot me through the heart. Goodbye. Give my love to the children. Bury me at Putney.'

Dr Nelson Johnston was sent for from his surgery on Mile End Road. As he crossed Sidney Street a bullet buzzed past him, and only after a difficult and dangerous journey over walls and low roofs was he able to get to Leeson. Dr Johnston treated the wounds as best he could but he knew if Leeson was to stand a chance of survival he had to be taken to hospital. What followed was a brave evacuation of Leeson by stretcher as the shots continued to ring out, pinging off masonry, shattering plaster and windows and whizzing through the air. As they reached the last roof the group, including Dr Johnstone and Detective Inspector Wensley, were pinned down by fire: the doctor was grazed by a bullet, however the still conscious Leeson was not going to allow his comrades to risk their lives anymore and he selflessly rolled off the

Portraits of the people involved, and scenes from, the Houndsditch Murders and Siege of Sidney Street.

stretcher and was assisted into the yard by officers below and removed to the London Hospital, where he later recovered from his wounds.

By this time about an hour had passed and still the bullets rang out. Wensley knew it was time for decisive action and sent word to his superiors and via the Home Office: Home Secretary Winston Churchill gave permission for troops to be despatched from the Tower and soon set off to apprise himself of the situation on Sidney Street in person.

A rifle platoon consisting of Lieutenant Ross, two NCOs and seventeen men of the Scots Guards were despatched from the Tower. Also present was the reporter J.P. Eddy, who recalled the soldiers arriving shortly after 10 a.m.:

> I can now recall their smart and businesslike appearance which they presented and the sense of confidence which they at once imparted. Boards intended for the display of newspaper posters were borrowed from newsagents, and on these the soldiers lay at each end of the street. They were quickly on the mark, firing diagonally at No. 100.

No4. Scots Guards Firing at House in Sidney St. where Houndsditch Assassins were.

Lying on newspaper advert boards, the Scots Guards fire at the 'Anarchist's Fort' at No. 100 Sidney Street.

To be precise, the Scots Guards were deployed three on the corner with Oxford Street, two at the end of Hawkins Street, two on Lindley Street corner and three at the Mile End Road end of Sidney Street. Guardsmen were also positioned in Mann & Crossman's brewery in the positions previously occupied by the police marksmen, as well as other buildings opposite or with clear sight of No. 100. The soldiers were soon pouring rapid fire into the second-floor rooms of No. 100, forcing those inside down to the first and ground floors, and by maintaining regular fire reduced those firing out to the occasional shot or burst of fire. Between 11 a.m. and 12 noon the soldiers were augmented by a further sixty police armed with shotguns and revolvers. A gunsmith also arrived with his stock of shotguns and ammunition, which was handed out to those police officers with military experience.

The scene was well observed by reporters, a number of whom (including J.P. Eddy and Philip Gibbs, later knighted for his work as a correspondent during the First World War) had paid a sovereign to the enterprising landlord of the nearby Rising Sun public house for a commanding view of the street. Indeed, Gibbs was later to recall: 'On that morning when Eddy and I stood under fire-bullets were ricocheting off the walls around us – we were, I remember, extraordinarily careless of any danger.' Another reporter present was Joseph Meaney, who was so proud of the bullet hole through the tail of his overcoat that he refused to have it mended.

The *Daily Chronicle* reporter evocatively recorded what he saw from the roof as the gunmen exchanged fire with the Guards:

Carefully does it: Scots Guards marksmen choose their moment from their vantage point in a building opposite No. 100 Sidney Street.

The police and soldiers doing their duty on Sidney Street: note the nurse on stand-by in the crowd and the locals and newspaper reporters gathering on the window ledges.

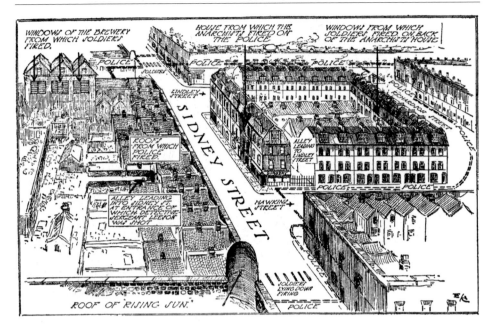

Plan of the Siege of Sidney Street.

Bullets were raining upon it [No. 100]. As I looked I saw how they spat at the walls, how they ripped splinters from the wall, how they made neat grooves as they burrowed into the red bricks, or chipped off corners of them. The noise of battle was tremendous and almost continuous. The heavy barking reports of army rifles were followed by the sharp and lighter cracks of pistol shots. Some of the weapons had a shrill singing noise, and others were like children's pop guns. Most terrible and deadly in sound was the rapid fire of the Scots Guards, shot speeding on shot, as though a Gatling gun were at work. Then there would come a sudden lull, as though a bugle had sounded 'cease fire,' followed by a silence, intense and strange, after the ear-splitting din.

It reopened again when a few moments later there came the spitting fire of an automatic pistol… From my vantage point I could see how the assassins changed the position from which they fired. The idea that only two men were concealed within that arsenal seemed disproved by the extreme rapidity with which their shots came from one floor and another. As I watched, gripped by the horror and drama of it, I saw a sharp stabbing flash break through the garret window. The man's weapon must have been over the edge of the window sill. He emptied his magazine, spitting out the shots at the house opposite, from which picked marksmen of the Scots Guards replied with instant volleys. A minute later by my watch shots began to pour through the second floor window, and before the echo of them had died away there was a fusillade from the ground floor.

So this amazing duel went on, as a distant clock chimed the quarters and half hours. From 11 o'clock until 12.30 there were not scores or hundreds of shots fired, but thousands. It seemed the assassins had an almost inexhaustible supply of ammunition.

Home Secretary Winston Churchill (furthest forward man wearing a top hat) comes to see the 'Battle of Stepney' for himself.

At around noon Winston Churchill, the Home Secretary, arrived and took up a position on the corner of Hawkins Street, less than 100 yards from the fighting. He was apprised of the situation and discussed plans for breaking the siege with the senior officers present. Suggestions of breaking through the walls of the adjoining property or dropping through the roof into No. 100 were considered. Churchill himself thought a search should be made of local foundries for a large steel plate which could cover officers as they rushed the building; another story told of a suggestion to bring in a field gun and pound the building to the ground.

But all these discussions were to be proved purely academic when, shortly after 1 p.m., the cry of 'Fire!' was heard from among the onlookers. Smoke and a lick of flame were spotted coming out of a garret window and within minutes the flames came through the roof as the house went up like a tinder box. Station Officer Edwards, in charge of the Bethnal Green fire engine, arrived at the scene, but was stopped by police. At Churchill's personal intervention they were ordered to stand fast. Within the hour the house had been engulfed in flames and smoke; soon the roof and floors collapsed within, sending masonry and burning timbers showering onto the street.

At this stage it was almost certain that no one could have survived the inferno. Detectives, revolvers in hand, cautiously approached No. 100. One of them kicked the door in: he was met by a wall of fire and a belch of flame. Further checks were made that none of the 'anarchists' had broken through the adjoining walls before the fire brigade was finally allowed to train their hoses on the fire and douse the flames. But even then No. 100 was a house of death, for as a party of firemen moved in to

At 1 p.m. the cry of 'Fire!' was heard from among the onlookers on Sidney Street as smoke and a lick of flame were spotted coming out of a garret window.

Once it was almost certain that no one could have survived the fire, detectives, revolvers in hand, cautiously approached No. 100.

The fire brigade are finally allowed to train their hoses on the fire and douse the flames. But even then No. 100 was still a house of death for as a party of firemen moved in to begin the sift of the debris part of the building collapsed injuring five firemen – one of them fatally.

begin sifting through the debris, part of the building collapsed, injuring five firemen – one of them, Charles Pearson, fatally.

Among the cinders of the fire-scorched remnants, the bodies of those believed to be Svaars and Joseph were discovered. The remains of Svaars still had his Mauser pistol close by (this relic was later displayed at the headquarters of the City Police at Old Jewry). Joseph was discovered among the debris of the collapsed first floor. He was known to have walked with a pronounced limp, and when his bones were uncovered they were deduced to be his as 'the shaft of the femur showed a circular elevation – probably the site of a former fracture.' This relic was displayed at the Medico-Legal Collection of the Royal College of Surgeons of England, but is believed to have been destroyed after the bombing of the building where the collection was housed in 1941.

So ended the Siege of Sidney Street, also known as the Battle of Stepney. The international press, who clearly had no understanding of the climate of fear surrounding anarchists, which, rightly or wrongly, had built up in London, spoke of overkill. The captured gang members identified as being involved in the Houndsditch Murders were brought to trial, but were faced by weak cases against them and the charges failed to stick; the men walked free. Nina Vassilleva faced two years imprisonment with hard labour for harbouring a felon, but even this was quashed by the court of appeal on the grounds of misdirection of the jury by the judge.

A policeman guards the entrance to the burnt-out shell of No. 100 Sidney Street.

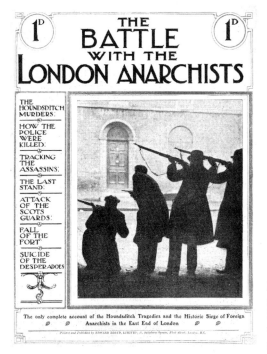

Postcards, photographs, newspapers and supplements recording the Siege of Sidney Street sold in their thousands – 'The Battle with the London Anarchists' is a rare surviving example. (*Steward P. Evans*)

CITY OF LONDON POLICE.

MURDER OF POLICE OFFICERS.

£500 REWARD

WHEREAS Sergeants Charles Tucker and Robert Bentley, and Constable Walter Charles Choat, of the City of London Police, were murdered in Exchange Buildings, in the said City, at 11.30 p.m., on the 16th December, 1910, by a number of persons who were attempting to feloniously break and enter a Jeweller's Shop, and killed the officers to prevent arrest, and whereas, THREE PERSONS whose descriptions, etc., are given below, are wanted for being concerned in committing the said crime, viz. :

FIRST. A MAN known as PETER PIATKOW, alias SCHTERN, alias "PETER THE PAINTER," age 28 to 30 years, height 5 feet 9 or 10 inches, complexion sallow, clear skin, hair and medium moustache black, otherwise clean shaven, eyes dark, medium build, reserved manner. Dress, brown tweed suit (broad dark stripes), black overcoat (velvet collar rather old), black hard felt hat, black lace boots, rather shabby. A native of Russia, an Anarchist.

PORTRAIT OF THE SAID PETER PIATKOW.

SECOND.—A MAN who gave the name of JOE LEVI, probably false, age 27 to 29 years, height 5 feet 6 or 7 inches, hair dark, supposed clean shaved, complexion somewhat pale, full round face, thickish lips, medium build, erect carriage. Dress, black overcoat, dark tweed cap. Foreign appearance, speaks fairly good English.

THIRD.—A WOMAN, age 26 to 30 years, height 5 feet 6 or 7 inches, fairly full breasts, sallow complexion, face somewhat drawn, eyes blue, hair brown. Dress, dark three-quarter jacket and skirt, large black hat (trimmed black silk), light-coloured shoes. Foreign appearance.

The above reward of £500 will be paid by the Commissioner of Police for the City of London to any person who shall give such information as shall lead to the arrest of these three persons, or in proportion to the number of such persons who are arrested.

Information to be given to the City Police Office, 26, Old Jewry, London, E.C., or at any Police Station.

City Police Office,
26, Old Jewry, London, E.C.
30th January, 1911.

J. W. NOTT BOWER,
Commissioner of Police for
the City of London.

WERTHEIMER, LEA & CO., Printers, Worship Street, London, E.C.

After the battle the search continued for the elusive and enigmatic 'Peter the Painter'.

Still, some shadowy gang members were believed to remain at large, but only one truly caught the public's imagination – Peter Piatkow, alias the enigmatically named 'Peter the Painter' (this nickname came from his work as a painter and decorator, not because he was a man known for any real artistic inclinations). Undoubtedly a member of the gang, his role and significance within it has become exaggerated out of all proportion. Like infamous predecessors Spring-Heeled Jack and Jack the Ripper, the mystique of 'Peter the Painter' caught the moment through a heady blend of his involvement with criminal acts of national concern and his strong, handsome features which adorned many a wanted poster and newspaper. Spiced with the 'exotic' mystery of his past life and travels across Europe, the public's fascination with this tall, dark and mysterious man endured – he even had a certain seductive appeal, particularly among certain young and impressionable women drawn to bad men.

As a consequence, the media interest lingered on him. Because of the intense public interest, newspaper reports scrabbled for news of sightings and supposed narrow escapes, adding yet more to his air of daring and mystery. This elusive 'Scarlet Pimpernel' character acquired quite a folk-hero status, and despite his name being on many lips – and being sought here and sought there – he was never caught.

Heroes of the Siege of Sidney Street gather for the camera.

Another crime persistently entangled with the Houndsditch Murders and Siege of Sidney Street is the murder of Leon Beron, a Russian Jew who had come to Whitechapel from France and was beaten to death with a blunt object, probably an iron bar or 'burglar's jemmy'. He was also stabbed and robbed. His body was found among bushes on Clapham Common at about 7.30 a.m. on New Year's Day in 1911. This association was made more acute as accounts of Beron's murder appeared cheek by jowl with the reports of the Siege of Sidney Street, and one of the senior investigating officers was Inspector Wensley (who had led the investigation of the Houndsditch Murders and had a high-profile role at the Sidney Street siege). The temptation to find some association between the crimes was irresistible. Beron's killer was in fact a convicted burglar on ticket-of-leave named Steinie Morrison (29), and it was far more likely that he was motivated more by greed than politics and killed Beron for his money.

However, certain mysteries remained, notably the curious 'S' shapes cut into Beron's face. The conjecture over their supposed significance or symbolism was widely reported and discussed in the newspapers after the publication of the inquest findings. An exchange at the Central Criminal Court trial between Mr Edward Abinger, Morrison's tenacious defence counsel, and Joseph Needham, W Division's Police Surgeon, went as follows:

Abinger: Do you agree that the symmetrical cuts on the face were extraordinarily like two S's?

Needham: Yes, that is so. I think I described them as being rather like the 'f' holes of the violin, on each side of the strings.

The Illustrated Police News' cover story of the murder of Leon Beron.

Leon Beron.

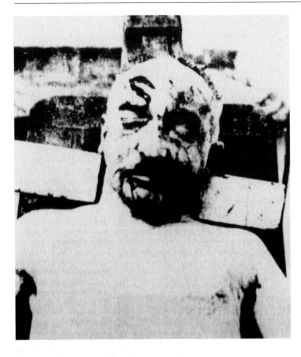

Post-mortem photograph of Beron:
note the impressions left about
his head from the blows of the
'burglar's jemmy'.

Abinger: What did you say in the Court below, dealing with these facial injuries?

Needham: They could not have been produced accidentally. They could not have been
caused by the face passing over something rough on the ground; they were cuts with a
knife... I thought it was extraordinary that anyone should have stopped to inflict such
wounds; they were not dangerous to life.

Abinger: Did you say that you thought they were some sign?

Needham: Yes, I said that at the Coroner's Court.

Abinger: Do you know the word 'spic,' which is Russian?

Needham: No.

Abinger: Meaning false spy?

Needham: No.

Abinger: Or 'spikan', the Polish word for spy?

Needham: No, at the time I knew nothing about it.

Abinger: Did you know the word 'Sorregio,' the Camorra sign?

The surgeon did not know this either, but commented he had since learnt of the
significance from the press. At this Mr Justice Darling brought the exchange to a
close by interjecting: 'We must not have this.' Detective Wensley also gave evidence
later at the trial and flatly denied Beron was a police informer.

But the seed was planted, and those apparently crudely-cut letters incised into each
of his cheeks became a clear suggestion, repeated in the press and by some subsequent
crime historians, that Beron was a spy and a police informer and one who gave up
members of the gang responsible for the Houndsditch Murders. Morrison, who had a

Steinie Morrison in the dock at the South-Western Police Court.

murky background and also probably came from Russia, stood trial in March 1911. Whether he carved the S's for a reason or not he never revealed. Either way, he was found guilty of the murder. A number of witnesses had placed Morrison in Beron's company on New Year's Eve, but the pivotal evidence against him came mostly from a driver who identified Morrison as the man he took in his cab from near the scene of the crime at the relevant time. Although convincing enough for the jury, the evidence was considered 'dubious' by the judge (who said as much in his summing up) and this view was shared by many others. After an appeal hearing, the matter was placed into the hands of the Home Secretary, who preferred not to intercede either way and recommended the exercise of Royal Prerogative. Morrison was given a prison sentence rather than face the gallows. Morrison then appealed against this judgement on no less than four occasions – *he* would rather swing than endure prison! The prison sentence remained, so did his grievance – year after year Morrison continued to protest by being a morose and difficult prisoner who went on successive hunger strikes. He died in Parkhurst Prison infirmary on 24 January 1921.

8

SECOND TIME AROUND

William Cronin (1897 & 1925)

The victory for the strikers in the Great Dock Strike of 1889 had established strong trade unions amongst London dockers, especially among the poorest unskilled casual labourers. Solidarity among the workers was shown to be the key to success and anyone who broke with those striking would be labelled a 'black leg' and frequently became prey to abuse, intimidation and violence, especially among the coal porters who were 'a tough breed and a strong element in the strike.' Almost ten years later, in July 1897, the river workmen came out on strike over pay.

Henry Cuthbert was the father of a young family who could not afford to strike. On the night of 23 July 1897 he went to the Richard Cobden beerhouse on Repton Street, Limehouse. Shortly before closing time Cuthbert was recognised by coal porter William Cronin (27) who called over, 'You are the man that works on the wood boats?' Cuthbert replied, 'Yes, anywhere to earn a shilling.' Cronin challenged him, 'you work for three shillings a day and others get five.' Cuthbert could sense Cronin was drawing attention and becoming aggressive; not wanting any trouble – and as the pub was soon closing – Cuthbert walked out the building and set off to return to his home at 16 Carr Street. But Cronin was fired up by his union fervour and the drink he had consumed and decided to follow.

Cuthbert's house was a short distance from the beerhouse and his wife Eliza had left the older children inside watching their baby as she went outside. She saw Cronin having words with her husband on the street: Cronin was shouting at Cuthbert about the strike – when he hit out at Cuthbert, Eliza ran over and Cronin also lashed out at her, striking her shoulder and sending her onto the ground. When she collected herself and got back inside her house, to her horror she discovered the baby she had left inside had been injured about the head. It was claimed that Cuthbert had gone into the yard of their house and was followed again by Cronin who, while in the yard, armed himself with an iron spade and strode into the Cuthbert's kitchen. He snarled 'First come first served!' Upon which he struck 10-month-old baby Eliza across the head with the spade.

Casually employed dockers waiting to see if there was any work for the day, *c.* 1896.

The West India dock as Cronin would have known it.

Gurney Ward at the London Hospital.

A police constable was nearby and Cronin was soon under arrest for maliciously cutting and wounding the child. He did come quietly – perhaps the sight of a uniform and the reality of his horrific actions sobered him up – and he said, 'All right governor, they set on me first.' At Thames Police Court, Constable A. Pinchin stated Cronin had said, 'I hope the child dies and I shall get hung.' The poor babe was rushed to the London Hospital, but sadly died.

Evidence showed that the baby had suffered a slight wound about 2½in long on the left side of the head which had cut through to the bone. The frontal bone was fractured. An operation was performed in an attempt to raise the depression, but the child died the following day from loss of blood and shock as a direct result of the injuries inflicted by Cronin. By the time of his appearance before the magistrate on 30 July, the coroner's jury had already returned a verdict against Cronin and the magistrate, Mr Dickinson, committed William John Cronin for trial on a charge of wilful murder.

Cronin appeared at the Central Criminal Court on 15 September 1897 before Mr Justice Bruce. Mr C.F. Gill and Mr Bodkin led for the prosecution but were no match for Mr E.P.S. Counsel who led a skilful defence bringing forward witnesses, notably Henry Corcoran who claimed he had seen Cuthbert attack Cronin with the spade first and suggested that the blow to the child's head had been caused accidentally during the scuffle. Cronin himself claimed he had never entered Cuthbert's house and claimed, at that time, he was with a Mary Farrow. The jury were certainly persuaded enough to believe that there were some grounds for reasonable doubt over Cronin's culpability for wilful murder, and he was found guilty of the lesser charge of manslaughter – a verdict that undoubtedly saved him from the gallows… for the time being.

Mr Justice Bruce had seen from Cronin's record that he had previously been convicted of assault and postponed judgement. On Friday 17 September 1897 Cronin was sentenced to seven years penal servitude.

Twenty-eight years later in 1925, when Cronin was 54, he was working as a ship's fireman living, when he was not away 'on the boats', at 126 Old Church Road, Stepney with Mrs Alice Garratt who had had met through visits to see his sister Emma Jane Sartain; Alice had lived on the floor below. Garrett was a widow, her husband had died the previous year and it was not long after that she and Cronin began living together.

Their relationship was one punctuated with quarrels so fierce they were overheard and the subject of concern among their neighbours. On the night of Friday 12 June 1925 one formidable row erupted between Cronin and Garratt. He claimed his sister had informed him that while he was away at sea Garratt had entertained other men, an accusation vehemently denied by Garratt (Cronin's sister also denied she made any such allegation about Garratt when later questioned about it in court.)

During the argument Garrett was heard to cry out 'Murder!' by William and Rose Blanks, who lived next-door at 128 Old Church Road. Deeply concerned, William Blanks went round to investigate and to his horror discovered 'Alice's head was hanging off'. Clearly in a state of shock, he returned to his waiting wife. Rose Blanks bravely went to investigate for herself. As she entered the house, Cronin pushed past her and made for the street. Aware that Cronin may well be attempting to make his getaway Alice followed him onto the street and shouted 'Stop him!' A passer-by named Charles James Edmead threw himself onto Cronin, eventually managing to pin him to the ground – but not before Cronin lashed out at him with a razor he was carrying, causing a nasty slash across one of Edmead's fingers. In the meantime William Blanks had gone in search of a constable and rapidly Cronin was arrested, restrained with hand cuffs and removed to the police station.

Cronin was remanded at Thames Police Court on Saturday 13 June 1925 and brought to trial at the Central Criminal Court on Friday 17 July before Mr Justice Swift. Cronin was defended by Mr W.A.L. Raeburn, who stood little chance against the strong evidence so eloquently presented against his client by the prosecuting counsels, Mr Percival Clarke and Mr G.D. Roberts. The jury did not leave its box to return the unanimous verdict of 'guilty', and Cronin was sentenced to death – to which Cronin contemptuously retorted, 'Thank you sir. I am very glad that you have sentenced an innocent man to death.'

On Thursday 30 July 1925 Cronin's appeal against the death sentence was heard. The Lord Chief Justice in giving the judgement of the court said,

> the defence raised at the trial was that a man other than Cronin had committed the crime while he (Cronin) was asleep... When Mrs Garrett was found dead her little children were also found asleep in the same bed. Attention had been drawn to various passages in the summing up but there was nothing of an adverse character to be said about the direction of the judge. It had been complained that the jury had come to their conclusion

in two minutes but it would have been more a matter of comment if the jury had taken longer to arrive at the very proper conclusion which they had expressed.

The appeal was dismissed and the Home Secretary decided he was unable to advise any interference with the sentence of death. William John Cronin shared the gallows with another (unassociated) murderer, Arthur Henry Bishop (18), in a double execution carried out by Robert Baxter, assisted by Henry Pollard, Edward Taylor and Robert Wilson at Pentonville Prison on Friday 14 August 1925.

9

AXE MURDER AT THE PALACE

John Frederick Stockwell, 1934

Monday 6 August 1934 was very much like any other Monday at the Eastern Palace Cinema (later re-named the Regal Cinema), which stood opposite Bow Church on the Bow Road. The last of the evening features crackled to an end, the crowd stood and left and the air was filled with a hubbub of chat, cigarette smoke and the sound of the squeak and thud of hundreds of velour-covered seats filled the air as the auditorium emptied for the night. Cinema manager Mr Dudley Henry Hoard (40) and his wife Maisie, somewhat weary from the day, retired to their flat above with their Persian cat Minnie. Dudley Hoard had enjoyed a lifetime in theatre; he had left school to perform at Sadlers Wells and then toured playing in pantomime, revue and drama and met his wife, a native of Newcastle-on-Tyne, when touring with the same company. After serving with the London Regiment during the First World War, Mr Hoard produced pantomimes at Liverpool and further productions around the country but decided to give up the demanding touring theatre life and enter the cinema business, learning the trade in Nottingham and eventually returning to London as the live-in manager at the Palace in March 1934 – probably not the dream of their own names in lights over the door, but they were happy.

Early on the morning of Tuesday 7 August the cleaning ladies were perturbed to find the doors of the cinema still locked. They had to wait for a key holder to let them in to start work – but when inside, to their horror, they discovered a trail of blood on the stairs to the upper circle which led to the partially clothed and bloody body of Dudley Hoard on the balcony. Another cleaner bravely followed the gory trail back up to the Hoard's flat, where the body of Mrs Maisie Hoard was discovered in her night attire. She too had been battered about the head – both victims had suffered horrific injuries inflicted by what was initially described as 'a blunt instrument' but showed signs of life, although both were unconscious. The police and ambulance were summoned and the Hoards removed to St Andrew's Hospital where Mr Hoard died shortly afterwards without regaining consciousness. However, Mrs Hoard rallied and, despite her injuries, she regained consciousness and managed to talk to the detectives at her hospital bedside. She gave a brief description of her assailant and was confident she would recognise him again. By the evening the hospital authorities issued a statement that 'Mrs Hoard was progressing favourably and every hope of her recovery was entertained.'

Detectives investigating the crime scene soon found evidence of a desperate struggle between Mr Hoard and his assailant. His slippers spoke volumes: the leather uppers and soles were coloured by the distemper on the walls of the staircase which led to the balcony where his body was found – looking at the marks, gouges and bloodstains along the walls of those stairs it was clear Dudley Hoard had fought violently up every one of those thirty stairs. Mr David Weinberg, joint owner of the cinema, knew Mr Hoard would have 'fought like a tiger', and Mr Hoard's father stated, 'My son was tall and very strong and not one to give in.' One silent witness was poor Minnie the cat, who was seen around the cinema in a state of terror, her coat matted, probably with blood, and limping as if she had been kicked.

The detectives faced a mystery – who did it? Was it one man, two or a gang? Did they get in by deception, hiding in the cinema or just break in? One thing was soon clear: the motive. The safe had been ransacked and emptied of a sum thought to be about £100.

After a late-night conference on 7 August, detectives decided to concentrate on tracing the owner of a waterproof coat which had been found in the sitting room of the flat. The investigating officers were satisfied the coat had not been the property of the Hoards and 'on one cuff of the coat some hair was noticed and the sleeves were pulled inside out', a clear indication the garment had been wrenched off the assailant's back during the struggle.

At 1 a.m. on Wednesday 8 August, Scotland Yard issued the following statement:

The manager of the cinema was attacked by a man who probably concealed himself on the premises and from whom he received injuries from which he has since died. His wife also received head injuries probably caused by blows with a hammer and is now in hospital. She is expected to recover. The key of a safe is missing from the flat and a sum of money is missing from the manager's office. The man who is described as being 22 years of age, 5ft 10in or over, complexion pale, clean shaven, long, dark hair, dressed in a dark suit and no hat is believed to have left the cinema by an exit door at the rear at about 4.30 a.m. on 7 August.

It is possible he hired a taxi-cab near the scene of the crime. His clothing is probably considerably bloodstained. The police will be glad of any information from the public which is likely to assist in the inquiries.

The following day, Wednesday 8 August, saw another piece towards solving the puzzle announced in the press. Detectives conducting a search of wasteland outside the back of the cinema discovered the murder weapon – a short hatchet with stains of blood on its edge (in later accounts and in court it was stated the axe was found in a lumber room behind the stage in the cinema). A bloody thumb print known not to be that of Mr Hoard was also discovered on the stairs. In the days before simple 'lift off' adhesive tape to remove fingerprints for analysis and preservation as evidence, police had no option other than to carefully chip out and remove 'about a square foot' of the plaster that contained the print. A piece of rubber flooring bearing two imprints of hand and footprints was also removed from the stalls for examination. Discovered immediately below the front of the balcony, it was suggested that perhaps this indicated Mr Hoard's killer had jumped or was forced from the balcony by his victim and fell the 20ft below – thus denying the attacker a *coup de grace*, Mr Hoard stumbled some way back towards the stairs but collapsed and passed out through loss of blood and shock.

This was also the day the police informed Mrs Hoard of her husband's death, an announcement made all the more bitter when it was discovered that the day also marked the couple's wedding anniversary.

Newspaper reports went on to state:

> The opening hour of the cinema was delayed while Scotland Yard cameramen took photographs of various parts of the building. A long queue waited outside. When the doors were finally opened it was announced that no seats could be occupied in the upper circle and the balcony which have been closed by the police.

But, in this case, the arm of the law was reaching powerfully in the direction of one man – the man recognised by Mrs Hoard, a man she knew by sight and name from before the attack. Over 9–10 August the suspect's name, photograph and detailed description were circulated to police and press across the country:

> Aged 19, height 5ft 7 or 8in., complexion pale, hair light brown, fairly long, parted at the side, eyes brown, long face. When last seen was wearing a dark brown suit, cream coloured shirt, with soft collar to match, and brown shoes. He seldom wears a hat or cap and has a small camera.

Friday 10 August saw the inquest opened at Poplar Coroner's Court with Dr R.L. Guthrie, coroner, presiding. Particular sympathy was recorded for Dudley Hoard's elderly mother, 'a small white-haired lady, who leaned heavily on the arm of a daughter.' Murmurs of sympathy were heard from across the court as these two figures, dressed all in black, passed into the tiny oak-panelled court-room.

After giving her son's details and confirming he was her only son, Mrs Hoard was asked if he had any enemies. She replied 'there were two men he had to dismiss when he was at Camden Town'. He had done so on the instruction of the proprietor because of the expense; she though they may have held a grudge because, 'These two men had wives and children', but she could not recall who they were. When the culprit of the murder was revealed it was clear these men were not involved.

Dr Temple Gray, the pathologist, in giving his statement of findings, confirmed Mr Dudley Hoard's death had been 'due to shock and haemorrhage, multiple scalp wounds and fractures of the skull.' Gray believed Mr Hoard had been struck down from behind but had got up again and pursued his assailant; 'I think he was then seized by the throat and his head dashed against a stone wall... there is evidence of a tremendous struggle. He must have been a powerful man.'

Hoping 'this wilful and callous murder' would soon be solved the coroner formally adjourned the hearing until 14 September. The following day Mr Hoard's body was removed from the Poplar Mortuary to the home of his mother at Croydon; he was later buried in Croydon cemetery.

Meanwhile the investigation of the murder case and the country-wide manhunt were soon to be concluded, but under truly bizarre circumstances. A letter was received at an address in East London from the wanted man in which he claimed the police would suspect he had something to do with the 'London cinema affair' and that he intended to change his name to 'Jack Barnard'. He gave his address as a lodging house in Lowestoft. This letter was soon in the hands of the police. On the morning of Wednesday 9 August the face of the wanted man was all over the national press and Mrs Alice Tripp, the keeper of the lodging house – who already had her suspicions aroused from the man's manner upon arrival – had her suspicions confirmed that he was the London cinema murderer and contacted the police. The information from both sources arrived at Lowestoft Police almost simultaneously and officers were soon at Mrs Tripp's lodging house. Searching his room they found a bloodstained suit, shirt and collar – but no suspect. Mrs Tripp had only read the paper after he had left, saying he was off to Yarmouth for the day.

Then, that same day, a locally postmarked letter was received by Lowestoft Police in Suffolk, addressed to the station inspector. It read:

Dear Sir
By the time you get this letter I shall be dead as I am going to drown myself. I want to confess to attacking Mr and Mrs Hoard at 7.40 a.m. on Tuesday. I am very sorry I killed him, as I did not intend to. I am writing you this as I cannot possibly go on any longer. I do not get any sleep as a picture haunts my brain and I cannot face the ordeal of a trial.

He then sent his love and sympathy to his sweetheart Miss Roake, continuing,

I hope she will forgive me. Sir, would you be so kind as to see that she gets the 30s which is to my credit in the P.O. book. I cannot go into details. I cannot bear to think of it. I am sorry for what I have done.
(signed) J.F. Stockwell

John Frederick 'Johnny' Stockwell, one of the Bow Road cinema attendants, was the man named by the police as 'wanted' to assist with their enquiries into the cinema murder – indeed, he was their number one suspect. His clothes were discovered neatly piled up on a lonely section of Lowestoft beach, his wrist watch and the post-office book mentioned in the pitiful letter among them. The problem with this apparent 'suicide' was that the subterfuge itself was pitiful. The section of the beach proved not to be as secluded as the killer thought and a holidaymaker out for an early morning stroll found the clothes little more than moments after they were left there. The letter had clearly been posted *after* the clothes were discovered. So, either a naked man walked across town and posted the letter and then waded into the water and drowned himself, or he just dumped the clothes there, changed into another suit and just walked away – but surely he would not have been foolish enough to go just where he told his landlady he was going?

On the afternoon of that same day a young man walked into The Metropolitan Hotel in Great Yarmouth and signing his name in the register as 'J.F. Smith, 138 London Road, Luton, Hertfordshire.' The hotel manager found it rather odd that a man who claimed to live there would not have known that Luton is in Bedfordshire. Again, the young man had aroused the suspicions of the manager, and he too contacted the police with his suspicions the following morning. Great Yarmouth police were soon on the scene and arrested 'Smith' – it was Johnny Stockwell. On the way to the police station – after complaining, 'Don't hold me so tight' – the man confessed, 'My name is Stockwell, not Smith. I know I am wanted for robbery.' When questioned about the murder, he admitted, 'Every bit of it is true; I am guilty of the crime.' Scotland Yard were informed and after a night and a morning in the cells at Yarmouth Borough police station, Stockwell was picked up at 1.50 p.m. on Saturday 11 August by Chief Inspector Sharpe. When cautioned, Stockwell replied: 'The only thing I can say is that I did not intend to kill him.'

He was driven back to London, escorted by Chief Inspector Sharpe and another officer. Only a small crowd of about thirty stood outside the Yarmouth police station as the car departed, but the news had got out and a large crowd of some 500 people awaited them in front of Bow Road police station, lining the route to the police yard gates three deep; the press recorded:

The car turned into Addington Street from the opposite end to that anticipated by the crowd, but there was still a rush to get a view of the occupants. In a few seconds the car, with drawn blinds, shot across the pavement and swung sharp right into the station yard and the gates promptly shut. The main doors of the police station were locked and constables posted at each corner of the building. Within minutes of his arrival Stockwell was formally charged and he was brought before Thames Police Court on Monday 13 August. Again, a large crowd awaited Stockwell's arrival on Charles Street and hoped to catch a glimpse of him but most were disappointed as the small saloon car drew up at the side entrance to the yard of the court and hustled in by a side door by a plain clothes officer. The proceedings at Thames Police Court were brief, the circumstances of the crime and arrest read out, Stockwell chose to remain silent; the officer beside him articulating Stockwell's request for legal aid and his wish to see some of his friends – both requests were granted and Stockwell was remanded until 21 August. The whole proceedings lasted less than five minutes.

The METROPOLITAN

MARINE PARADE
(CENTRAL)
GT. YARMOUTH

•

*Established
over 40 years.*

'*Phone:* Yarmouth 850.

Telegrams: Metropolitan 850 Gt. Yarmouth.

DINING-ROOM

Ideally situated in a most central position adjoining the Marine Parade, half-way between the two Piers, and overlooking the Bathing Pool and Sea.

Near Tennis Courts, Bowling Greens, Hippodrome and Cinemas.

Half-minute from main Motor Coach Terminus.

This popular well-known establishment has recently been entirely redecorated and extensively refurnished.

With its exceptionally fine position, 30 comfortable bedrooms (many with good sea view), spacious Dining-room and pleasant Lounge, together with a high standard of catering, comfort and service, offers exceptional value in holiday accommodation.

Pleasant sociable company and no petty restrictions.

ALL BEDROOMS FITTED WITH HOT AND COLD RUNNING WATER

Electric light throughout. Piano. Wireless. Baths (h. & c.). Mid-day Dinner. Four good meals daily. Varied menus. Large and small tables. Metropolitan Garage at rear.

•

Inclusive Terms from
49/- *per week.*

LOUNGE

MR. and MRS. C. LARWOOD - - - Proprietors

1934 advert for The Metropolitan Hotel, Marine Parade, Great Yarmouth, where the Palace Axe Murderer was finally arrested.

Marine Parade, Great Yarmouth in the mid-1930s.

Stockwell's next appearance heard the case and statement and his plea of 'not guilty'. At this hearing it was revealed Stockwell had deposited a case, in which was concealed £90 from the robbery, at Aldgate East Station. Chief Inspector Sharpe then referred to his notes and related a conversation he had with Stockwell in the car while travelling from Yarmouth to London. Quoting Stockwell, he stated:

> I first thought of doing this last Saturday. On Sunday night I found the axe in the yard where I was living – Leader's. When I went with my girl to the bus on Tuesday I carried the axe under my coat. I left her and went straight to the cinema. I got in by shaking the door at front and twisting the handle. I went to the flat, rang the bell, and Mr Hoard came to the door. I said 'I have left a ten-bob note in the hall – can I come in and look for it?' He said, 'Certainly.' He went to close the door when I pulled it open and tried to hit him with the axe. He ran into the room and I followed him, and hit him on the head with the axe from behind. He fell, and I hit him several times again with the axe. His wife came out of the bedroom and I hit her on the head with the axe. I don't know if I hit her on the ground.

Stockwell then seemed to wander into a strange account of how he tried to put Mr Stockwell on the bed and then took his keys, opened the safe and fled with the money – there was no mention of the death struggle on the stairs. Stockwell continued, 'I hid the axe behind the stage and went home.' He then related his movements and action until arrest at Great Yarmouth. Further evidence was presented, and Stockwell was ordered to appear at the Old Bailey. Throughout the proceedings Stockwell himself sat with his hands folded staring at the floor.

On Monday 23 October John Stockwell was brought before the Central Criminal Court; he appeared in the dock wearing an open-necked shirt. Mr Justice Goddard presided, the prosecution was led by Mr G.B. McClure (with Mr Eustace Fulton), and Mr Frederick Levy acted for the defence. Levy stated he had received written instructions and stated, 'Having examined the case from every aspect, the solicitor and himself felt it would be a lamentable farce to go through with the case to its bitter end with an inevitable result.' Stockwell changed his plea to 'guilty.'

The written instruction was given to the judge, who asked: 'is that your signature?'

Stockwell: Yes.

Judge: You understand what you are doing?

Stockwell: Yes.

Clerk of the Court: You have pleaded not guilty to this indictment. Do you wish to alter that plea?

Stockwell (with a firm voice): I do.

Clerk of the Court: What say you now?

Stockwell: Guilty, my Lord.

Mr Frederick Levy then addressed the jury with an impassioned plea to them for some recommendation of mercy in their verdict. In part of his address he said:

> You have before you a boy of 19 who from the age of 11 had no protected childhood. His father was killed in action when he was one year old and his mother died when he was 11. He was thrown upon the world and had to depend upon relatives... I ask the jury to do what they can to save this young man.

The judge did not direct the jury otherwise and when returning the verdict of 'guilty' also strongly recommended him to mercy. When asked if he had anything to say, Stockwell replied in a firm voice, 'I am deeply sorry for this tragedy.'

When addressing Stockwell, Justice Goddard pointed out he had accepted the change of plea because he was in the hands of an experienced counsel and because the judge had a report from the medical officer at Brixton Prison to certify his sanity. He then went on to state there was no doubt of Stockwell's guilt, but in conclusion, 'If any ray of light is to be found in this dark and tragic story, it is that by your confession and the course you are now taking you are showing some remorse for a crime as terrible as any recorded in the grim annals of this court.' He then pronounced sentence of death. Stockwell stood rigidly, as if at attention, as the words left the judge's lips, he then turned and walked firmly away as he was taken down.

Despite the recommendation for mercy and public concerns expressed about a boy of 19 facing the gallows there was to be no reprieve for Johnny Stockwell. He was hanged by Robert Baxter, assisted by Robert Wilson, at Pentonville Prison on Wednesday 14 November 1934.

10

MURDER AT THE BLIND BEGGAR

Ronald Kray, 1966

The Kray twins were born on 17 October 1933; the sons of Charles Kray (26), a dealer in second hand clothes, and his wife, Violet (21). With their older brother, Charlie, they spent much of their early life on Burdett Road, moving to Valance Road in Bethnal Green in 1939. Violet was a strong and loving mother, and as the boys grew up and got a reputation for fighting she was always quick to defend them, saying, 'It's never them what starts the trouble, but because they're twins they stand out and always get the blame.' As the twins matured they built up quite a business based around the protection racket – any trouble in pubs or snooker halls and the boys will 'sort it out' – for a fee of about £5 a night. Some publicans saw no point in paying for protection, but very soon they would be rushed by a gang of thugs who would attack customers with coshes and razors – and let's face it, that is bad for business.

The Kray brothers were canny businessmen too and with the money they soon amassed they took over the Regal billiard hall and a variety of clubs and bars, notably the Double R cabaret club (named after their initials) on Bow Road. They became local – and indeed, London – celebrities in their own right. The Krays were snappy dressers: wearing finely tailored Savile Row-style suits, they drove the latest Jaguar cars and were regularly featured in magazines and papers with stars of the time such as Diana Dors, Barbara Windsor and Freddie Mills. The boys were respected across the East End, they gave money to charitable organisations and many East Enders were to recall they felt safer 'and could leave their front door unlocked' when the Krays were in charge. Indeed, if you lived in the East End and were not part of the underworld scene you would have had little to fear from them: most folks knew what they were up to and would not 'mess them about'. The Kray boys doted on their Mum and respectfully called her 'our Queen'; at the height of their success in the mid-1960s anyone being less than respectful of Mrs Kray would soon regret their actions, as indeed would anyone getting above themselves on the Kray's 'manor' (or made adverse comments about the Krays themselves). Punishments meted out could range from beatings of varying degrees of violence or branding with a hot iron to a quick slash across the face or buttocks with a razor – as Ronnie said, 'so every time the bastards sit down they remember me.'

But some pushed too far, among them George Cornell. Cornell had grown up on the streets of the East End and was a hard man, 6ft tall, well built, handy with his fists. He had a reputation for taking a sadistic pleasure in violence and had served a prison term for slashing a woman's face. He had married skilful shoplifter Olive Hutton and moved to the Elephant and Castle, and by the mid-1960s had become a tough enforcer for the Richardson brothers and was suspected by Scotland Yard of being a contract killer. The old story which keeps being regurgitated is that Cornell had developed an unhealthy (for him) contempt for the Krays and had called Ronnie a 'fat poof'. According to 'Mad' Frankie Fraser, Ronnie Kray and others involved at the time, this was not the case. Although Ronnie did admit later in life that he was bisexual, at the time if someone had called Ronnie such a name it would have been seen as an insult, pure and simple, and Cornell would have been, in the eyes of gangland, justifiably 'chinned' there and then. Fraser recalls Cornell was often used as 'middle man' in negotiations between the Richardsons and the Krays. On one occasion he had been approached by the Krays about 'a job' but Cornell felt it just could not be done. As the Krays pressed him to join the scheme, he disrespectfully told them to 'fuck off' and angered Ronnie. If Ronnie had lashed out against Cornell at that moment reprisals from the Richardsons could well have led to an all-out gang war, so Ronnie bided his time.

In *Murders of the Black Museum* Gordon Honeycombe states that by 1966 an all-out gang war existed between the Krays and the Richardsons; attempts had been made on the lives of the Krays, and their cousin, Richard 'Dickie' Hart, had been gunned down during a shoot-out between the Richardsons and a local gang at the Mr Smith and the Witchdoor bar in Catford. Reprisals were called for to avenge the death of Hart – 'one of theirs for one of ours'. Most of the Richardsons had been sent down as a result of the Catford shooting – with the exception of Cornell, who was not present at the club shooting – so Cornell no longer had the backup of the Richardsons and Ronnie was not going to forget the disrespect he had been shown.

On the evening of 9 March 1966 news reached the Krays that George Cornell had brazenly walked onto their 'manor' and was having a drink in The Blind Beggar pub on the Mile End Road. In fact, Cornell and his pal Albie Woods had been to the hospital to visit Jimmy Andrews, who had lost his leg in a shooting, and had called in to The Blind Beggar for a drink on the way back.

When they received the telephone call informing them about Cornell, the Krays were drinking with some of their 'firm' at 'The Widow's' on Tapp Street (real name The Lion, but so nicknamed after the landlady's husband had died). Reg suggested they talk about their actions, but Ronnie had made his mind up – taking Reggie's driver, John 'Scotch Jack' Dickson, and Ian Barrie they drove over to The Blind Beggar in their Ford Cortina, picking up shooters on the way. When they arrived

Dickson stayed with the car as Kray and Barrie entered the pub at about 8.30 p.m. Accounts vary between twelve and thirty people being in the pub at the time (one man I knew personally said he was drinking in the pub on the night in question and was urged 'by a friend' not to be around – no names were mentioned but he was left in no doubt 'something was going to happen' and left quick sharp. He only learnt about the events of the night before when he read the morning papers). Cornell and Woods were sitting at the bar on stools and had ordered light ales. Cornell turned to see who had come in, then realising who it was sneered and said sarcastically, 'Well, look who's here.' Ronnie was now at point blank range, and without saying a word – and with one smooth motion – he drew the 9mm Mauser automatic pistol he was carrying from the shoulder holster concealed beneath his jacket and shot Cornell once in the forehead, just above his right eye, turned on his heels and exited just as calmly as he strode in. Cornell slumped onto a column and slid down, dying, to the floor. As the ringing in the barmaid's and customer's ears died down and they began to compose themselves after the shock of what had happened, they noticed that the juke box – which had been playing the Walker Brothers hit 'The Sun Ain't Gonna Shine Anymore' – was stuck on the words 'Anymore… Anymore… Anymore.'

Within ten minutes detectives were on the scene, but, of course, no one had seen anything: the line was that Cornell was the only customer and the bar staff were all out the back at the time of the shooting. There was even a line up, including Ronnie Kray, at Commercial Street police station, but the barmaid failed to recognise anyone as the killer, explaining she had 'a bad memory for faces.'

Reggie Kray followed his brother's path to murder with the killing of troubled gangland character Jack 'the Hat' McVitie – named after the pork-pie hat he always wore to cover his baldness. McVitie had been hired to carry out an assassination on behalf of the Krays but had failed to do so and had not paid back the money. He compounded his troubles by making offensive and derisory comments about the Krays which got back to the ears of the brothers. In November 1966 McVitie was brought from the Regency Club in Stoke Newington to what he thought was another party at a flat on Evering Road, Hackney. Ron and Reg were waiting for Jack, and Reggie wasted no time pointing a pistol at point-blank range at McVitie. He pulled the trigger. Nothing happened. Reg attempted to fire again and again, only to be met with 'click' after 'click.' McVitie thought he was the butt of some sick joke, but he laughed no more as Ron held him and Reg stabbed him in the face, stomach and finally impaled him through the throat on the floor. Wrapped in a bedspread, the dead body of McVitie was bundled into a car and was never seen again.

The third killing attributed to the Krays was that of Frank 'Mad Axeman' Mitchell – a body-builder and giant of a man who was 6ft 4in and weighed 17 stone. A real East End hard man, he was a daring criminal but the problem was that he was mentally 'backward', prone to childish tantrums and kept getting caught. When in custody and brought before the courts he had been assessed and declared 'mentally defective' with 'the mind of a 10-year-old child' by the authorities and had served sentences at Rampton and Broadmoor. Ron and Reg had met Mitchell when they

Ron and Reg Kray at home having a cup of tea. They had just spent 36 hours being questioned by the police about the murder of George Cornell. (Hulton Archives/Getty Images)

were in Wandsworth and he had kept in touch with Ron and was frustrated that he was constantly denied a review date for his case. He was already a trusted prisoner at the Dartmoor open prison; security was low and with a little planning his escape on 12 December 1966 was made possible by the Krays. The escape was headline news. Once out, Mitchell had to lie low and was put up in a flat on Barking Road, East Ham, guarded by Scotch Jack Dickson and Billy Exley and entertained by night-club hostess Lisa Prescott. But Mitchell became impatient and within days had sent letters in his childish scrawl to *The Times* and *Daily Mirror* asking the Home Secretary for a release date. He was also demanding to see the Krays – saying if they did not come to him he would go to them. Frankly, for the Krays, Mitchell had become a liability. Reg paid him a visit and said they would move him to the country. He was removed in a van on Christmas Eve and was never seen again: he is still classified as a wanted man on the run by the police. However, former Kray firm member Freddie Foreman, in his autobiography *Respect*, claimed that Mitchell was shot and the body disposed of in the sea. When firm member 'Scotch Jack' Dickson asked Ronnie what had happened to Mitchell, Ronnie flew into a rage shouting, 'He's fucking dead! We had to get rid of him, he would have got us all nicked. We made a mistake getting the bastard out in the first place.'

It must be remembered that the police had made great efforts to bring the Krays to justice and Inspector Leonard 'Nipper' Read of Scotland Yard was the man determined to bring them down. He had been investigating their activities since 1964, but was often hindered by the wall of silence from the people too afraid of what may happen to them if they gave up the twins. By the end of 1967 Read had built up evidence against the Krays. There were witness statements incriminating them, as well as other evidence, but they did not add up to a convincing case on any one charge. Most of the statements were given on the condition that they were not used until the Krays were in detention, making a warrant almost impossible to obtain.

But slowly and surely, Inspector Read and his team assembled a case against the Krays. They were finally were arrested on 9 May 1968. Once they were detained in police custody, witnesses slowly started to develop the confidence to give evidence and twenty-eight criminals were promised freedom from prosecution if they were to turn Queen's Evidence against the Krays – the criminals involved had much to lose and could face a life behind bars, the temptation was great and even close Kray gang members such as Scotch Jack Dickson and Ronnie Hart gave their testimony. Witnesses such as the barmaid at The Blind Beggar recovered their memories.

The Kray trial was a sensation; held at the Old Bailey before Mr Justice Melford Stevenson, it commenced on 8 January 1969 and saw the Kray brothers tried together, with a further eight members of their firm. The trial lasted thirty-nine days (then the longest and most expensive trial held at the London court).

Ronnie arrogantly denied everything, called the prosecutor 'a fat slob', said the police had plotted against him and his brother and directly accused the judge of bias. On the final day of the trial, 4 March 1969, the jury deliberated for six hours and fifty-five minutes before unanimously returning a verdict of guilty against Ronnie Kray and John Barrie for the murder of George Cornell. Reg Kray was found guilty of the murder of Jack McVitie. The Kray's elder brother, Charlie, got ten years for helping with the disposal of McVitie's body Frederick Foreman and Cornelius Whitehead were also found guilty of being accessories to the murder of McVitie.

Christopher and Anthony Lambrianou and Ronald Bender were also found guilty of murder and received life. Frederick Foreman was jailed for ten years. Cornelius Whitehead was sentenced to seven years. Albert Donaghue was jailed for two years. The Kray twins were both sentenced to life imprisonment with a recommendation they should be detained for a minimum of thirty years.

On 15 April 1969, all three Krays were back in court facing charges of murdering Frank 'Mad Axeman' Mitchell. All pleaded not guilty, and despite evidence given against them by hostess Lisa Prescott and firm member Albert Donaghue, who claimed to have been in the van which took away Mitchell with Freddie Foreman and Alfie Gerrard – he recalled it took twelve shots to finally kill Mitchell – it remained impossible to prove who killed the Mad Axeman. The Krays were cleared of the murder, but Reg was convicted of plotting Mitchell's escape from Dartmoor Prison and got another five years.

Ronnie was eventually committed to Broadmoor Hospital, Crowthorne and died there on 17 March 1995. Charles Kray died in prison in April 2000 while serving time for masterminding a £69m cocaine smuggling plot. Reg was imprisoned for a total of thirty-two years before he was released from custody on compassionate grounds as a result of cancer, which claimed his life a few weeks after his release on 1 October 2000 at the Town House Hotel in Thorpe St Andrew, Norwich, Norfolk. On the day of his funeral the streets of the East End were filled with thousands of mourners, six deep along the Bethnal Green Road. Many shops closed as a mark of respect as his horse-drawn hearse, bedecked with floral tributes, passed by, closely followed by Kray's widow Roberta, close family members, former gangland 'enforcer', 'Mad' Frankie Fraser and many mourners. The cortege moved along the route via Valance Road to St Matthew's church where his funeral service was held and finally to Chingford Mount Cemetery where around 200 people accompanied the coffin to the grave where the last of the Kray brothers was finally laid to rest.

SELECT BIBLIOGRAPHY

BOOKS

Adam, H.L., *Trial of George Chapman* (Edinburgh & London 1930)

Begg, Paul and Skinner, Keith, *The Scotland Yard Files: 150 Years of the CID* (London 1992)

Booth, Charles, *Life and Labour of the People of London* (Vols I to IX London 1885–1905)

Eddy, J.P., *The Mystery of Peter the Painter* (London 1946)

Evans, Stewart P. and Skinner, Keith, *The Ultimate Jack the Ripper Sourcebook* (London 2000)

Fraser, Frankie, *Mad Frank: Memoirs of a Life of Crime* (London 1997)

Friedland, Martin L., *The Trials of Israel Lipski* (London 1984)

Honeycombe, Gordon, *The Murders of the Black Museum* (London 1982)

Irving, H.B., *Trial of the Wainwrights* (Edinburgh & London 1920)

Jackson, William, *The New and Complete Newgate Calendar or Malefactor's Universal Register* (London 1818)

Jones, G.S., *Outcast London* (Oxford 1971)

Lane, Brian, *The Murder Guide* (London 1991)

McCarthy, Terry, *The Great Dock Strike 1889* (London 1988)

Moulton, H. Fletcher, *Trial of Steinie Morrison* (London & Edinburgh 1922)

Oddie, S. Ingleby, *Inquest* (London 1941)

Ramsey, Winston G., *The East End Then and Now* (London 1997)

Ritchie, J. Ewing, *The Night Side of London* (London 1858)

Rumbelow, Donald, *The Houndsditch Murders & The Siege of Sidney Street* (London 1973)

Shew, E. Spencer, *A Companion to Murder* (London 1960)
Shew, E. Spencer, *A Second Companion to Murder* (London 1961)
Smith, Major Henry, *From Constable to Commissioner* (London 1910)
Storey, Neil R., *London: Crime, Death & Debauchery* (Stroud 2007)

NEWSPAPERS & PERIODICALS

Cassell's Saturday Journal
Daily Chronicle
East London Advertiser
East London Observer
Eastern Argus & Borough of Hackney Times
Evening Standard
Illustrated Police News
Pall Mall Gazette
Penny Illustrated Paper
The Eastern Post & City Chronicle
The Daily Mirror
The Illustrated London News
The Lancet
The Stage
The Star
The Strand Magazine
The Sun
The Times